Where are the *Girls*?

Girls in Fighting Forces in Northern Uganda, Sierra Leone and Mozambique: Their Lives During and After War

Susan McKay and **Dyan Mazurana**

Other publications by Rights & Democracy

A Methodology for Gender-Sensitive Research (1999).
Agnès Callamard, co-published with Amnesty International.

Investigating Women's Rights Violations in Armed Conflicts (2001).
Agnès Callamard in collaboration with Barbara Bedont, Ariane Brunet,
Dyan Mazurana and Madeleine Rees, co-published with Amnesty International.

Documenting Human Rights Violations by States Agents (1999).
Agnès Callamard, co-published with Amnesty international.

Securing Women's Rights to Land, Property and Housing: Country Strategies (2001).
Series of articles produced under the direction of Andina van Isschot.

Women & Peacebuilding (1999). Dyan E. Mazurana and Susan R. McKay.

*Only Silence Will Protect You. Women, Freedom of Expression
and the Language of Human Rights* (1996). Jan Bauer.

Where are the Girls?

Girls in Fighting Forces in Northern Uganda, Sierra Leone and Mozambique: Their Lives During and After War

Susan McKay and **Dyan Mazurana**

Rights & Democracy
International Centre for Human Rights and Democratic Development

Rights & Democracy
International Centre for Human Rights
and Democratic Development

Suite 1100, 1001 de Maisonneuve Blvd. East
Montréal, Québec
H2L 4P9 Canada
Tel.: (514) 283-6073/Fax.: (514) 283-3792/E-mail: ichrdd@ichrdd.ca
Visit our Web site: www.ichrdd.ca

Rights & Democracy (International Centre for Human Rights and Democratic Development) is a Canadian institution with an international mandate. It is an independent organization which promotes, advocates and defends the democratic and human rights set out in the International Bill of Human Rights. In cooperation with civil society and governments in Canada and abroad, Rights & Democracy initiates and supports programmes to strengthen laws and democratic institutions, principally in developing countries.

© International Centre for Human Rights and Democratic Development, 2004.

The opinions expressed in this book are the authors' own and do not necessarily reflect the views of Rights & Democracy. All rights reserved. No part of this publication may be reproduced in any form without prior permission from Right & Democracy (International Centre for Human Rights and Democratic Development).

Research and publication of this book were made possible with the financial support of the Government of Canada provided through the Canadian International Development Agency (CIDA).

 Canadian International   Agence canadienne de
Development Agency   développement international

Project Coordinator and Editor:
Ariane Brunet, Coordinator, Women's Rights, Rights & Democracy

English revision:
Janis Warne

Translation:
Claudine Vivier

Production and French revision:
Anyle Coté, Officer, Special Events & Publications, Rights & Democracy

Design:
Rouleau•Paquin Design Communication

Printed in Canada

Legal Deposit:
Bibliothèque nationale du Québec, first quarter, 2004.
National Library of Canada, first quarter, 2004.
ISBN: 2-922084-74-4

Table of Contents

Acronyms	6
Acknowledgements	7
Preface	9
Executive Summary	13
1 Where are the Girls?	17
2 Girls in Fighting Forces Worldwide, 1990–2003	21
3 War in Northern Uganda, Sierra Leone and Mozambique: Background and Overview	27
4 Comparative Findings of Psycho-spiritual, Physical and Psychological Health, and Sociocultural Issues	33
5 Northern Uganda, Sierra Leone and Mozambique: Girls' Entry and Experiences in Fighting Forces, Leaving the Forces and Disarmament, Demobilization and Reintegration	73
6 Conclusion	119
References	123
Appendices	
Appendix 1: Methodology	131
Appendix 2: Why Think About Girls in Fighting Forces?	139
Appendix 3: Interviews	141

Acronyms

AFRC	Armed Forces Revolutionary Council
AI	Amnesty International
AMODEG	Association of Demobilized Soldiers
CCF	Christian Children's Fund
CDF	Civil Defence Forces (Sierra Leone)
CIDA	Canadian International Development Agency
Coalition	Coalition to Stop the Use of Child Soldiers
CPA	Concerned Parents Association, Uganda
CPAR	Canadian Physicians for Aid and Relief
CPU	Child Protection Unit
DDR	Disarmament, Demobilization and Reintegration
DOL	US Department of Labor
ECOMOG	Economic Community of West African States Monitoring Group
ECOWAS	Economic Community of the West African States
FAWE	Forum of African Women Educationalists
FRELIMO	Frente de Libertação Nacional
GUSCO	Gulu Support the Children Organization
HRW	Human Rights Watch
IDP	Internally Displaced Person
ICC	Interim Care Centre
INGO	International Non-governmental Organization
IRC	International Rescue Committee
KICWA	Kitgum Concerned Women's Association
LDU	Local Defence Units
LRA	Lord's Resistance Army
NCDDR	Sierra Leone National Committee for Disarmament, Demobilization and Reintegration
NGO	Non-governmental Organization
NPFL	National Patriotic Front of Liberia
ONUMOZ	United Nations Operations in Mozambique
PHR	Physicians for Human Rights
RENAMO	Resistencia Nacional de Moçambique
RUF	Revolutionary United Front
RWC	Women's Commission for Refugee Women and Children
SBU	Small Boys Unit
SC	Save the Children
SGU	Small Girls Unit
SLA	Sierra Leone Army
STD	Sexually Transmitted Disease
STI	Sexually Transmitted Infection
TRC	Truth and Reconciliation Commission
UN	United Nations
UNAMSIL	United Nations Assistance Mission to Sierra Leone
UNHCR	United Nations Office of the High Commissioner for Refugees
UNICEF	United Nations Children's Fund
UNAMSIL	United Nations Assistance Mission to Sierra Leone
UNOMSIL	United Nations Observer Mission to Sierra Leone
UPDF	United People's Defence Force
WHO	World Health Organization
WV	World Vision

Acknowledgements

Susan McKay and Dyan Mazurana wish to thank the expert reviewers of the book manuscript, Courtney Mireille O'Connor and Michael Wessells. We greatly appreciated the support of Ariane Brunet of Rights & Democracy during the research process. At CIDA, we especially thank Gail Cockburn and Natalie Zend for overseeing this project so competently. Deep thanks also to Maggie Paterson and Diana Rivington for their support of our work from its beginning. External experts for this study were Laura Arntson, Neil Boothby, Kenneth Bush, Boia Effraime, Ilene Cohn, Elizabeth Jareg, Jean-Claude Legrand and Kathy Vandergrift. We consulted with each of them, some frequently, and we thank them for their insight and willingness to contribute to this study.

Dyan Mazurana wishes to thank and acknowledge her colleague Khristopher Carlson for his important contributions at every level of the work. Iain Levine also provided timely and insightful commentary. Colin Holtz provided excellent research assistance in collecting worldwide data. In Uganda, special thanks go to Dr. Frank Olyet and Angelina Acheng Atyam. In Sierra Leone, special thanks to Donald Robertshaw, Keith Wright, Glenis Taylor, Maurice Ellis and Michael Kamara. In Mozambique, deep thanks to Jose Correria and Joao Candido Pereira. Ellen and Steve Mazurana and Michael Young continue to provide support, including to the children of Northern Uganda, of which I am very grateful. Pat Bristol, Claire Carlson, GG Weix and Jill Belsky of the University of Montana, Ariane Brunet of Rights & Democracy and Maggie Paterson of CIDA helped in countless ways. For the Policy Commission study, I extend deep thanks to Sanam Anderlini and Ambassador Swanee Hunt.

Susan McKay wishes to thank the (almost) countless individuals who, through various ways, made the completion of this study possible. Many of these people are unnamed and helped greatly during fieldwork in Mozambique, Uganda and Sierra Leone. I especially thank my family, friends, and colleagues whose support was pivotal in my being able to complete this work. Also, I appreciate their financial support (and that of Laramie Zonta and Soroptimist service clubs in Laramie, Wyoming) in helping the children at the Makeni School for the Deaf in Sierra Leone.

Throughout the study, Janel Kasper was an extremely competent research assistant. She was responsible for gathering large amounts of background data and organizing it. Janel supervised the data coding process.

Maria Gonsalves was another highly valued research assistant who conducted fieldwork with me in Sierra Leone. Shay Cooper, Janel Kasper and Sarah Hoerle coded data during an intensive 6-week period from early November until mid-December 2002. Melissa Jaeger, Lindsay Stoffers, Sophia Berg and Elizabeth Lynch, undergraduate students at the University of Wyoming, assisted with data entry, printing and organizing data in notebooks. Dr. Sharon Cumbie of the School of Nursing generously supported my use of the nursing research centre's facilities and resources. Her help and that of other colleagues in the School of Nursing came at a critical point in the data analytic process. Denise Manore, administrative assistant in the Women's Studies program, gave cheerful assistance on many occasions. Wendy Starnes, formerly administrative assistant in Women's Studies, was similarly helpful during the first year of the study. Among other tasks, Denise and Wendy were responsible for the very time-consuming work of tracking the CIDA financial accounts. Cathy Connolly, director of the Women's Studies program, supported the study's completion in many important ways; I wish to thank her for bearing through (my) stress-filled days and for the substantive financial and administrative help of the program.

McKay's study findings were reviewed at various stages by the following individuals: Maria Gonsalves, Janel Kasper, Abubacar Sultan, Michael Wessells, Elizabeth Jareg, Binta Mansaray, Mary Burman, Susan Shepler, Ilene Cohn, Courtney Mireille O'Connor and Caroline Lamwaka. I am grateful for the expertise these people shared so fully. Five of these individuals— Mike, Elizabeth, Mary, Susan and Courtney—participated in several levels of review of the analytic findings, which was very time consuming for them.

Susan McKay owes particular thanks to Roger Wilmot of the U.W. Research Office and Rodney Lang of the U.W. Legal Office for their ongoing belief in the integrity and quality of my work and their support for its completion. Christy Rickard competently managed the Wyoming and Montana accounts. I also thank the University of Wyoming Graduate School, the Research Office, the Women's Studies Program, the Office of the Dean of Arts and Sciences, the International Studies Program, the Provost's Office, the School of Nursing and the Office of International Travel for their financial support of my work and this study.

Preface

At the beginning of the 1990s, the international community finally acknowledged the necessity of addressing the issue of women's human rights after having placed women and children together for far too long in a sub-category of human dignity. The Vienna Declaration and the Programme of Action of June 1993, which stemmed from the World Conference on Human Rights, urged all governments and the United Nations to make the "full and equal enjoyment by women of all human rights" a priority. A separate chapter was devoted to the rights of the child. It was an acknowledgement that women and children experience specific realities that cannot be lumped together and dealt with generically.

The Beijing Declaration and Platform for Action of the Fourth World Conference on Women in 1995 devoted an entire strategic objective to women and armed conflict. As a sign of the times, violence against women in armed conflict situations was specifically addressed. As noted in paragraph 135 of the Platform, "while entire communities suffer the consequences of armed conflict and terrorism, women and girls are particularly affected because of their status in society and their sex."

As stated in Security Council Resolution 1325 on Women, Peace and Security, they can also play an important role in the prevention and resolution of conflicts and in peace-building. However, in order to be acknowledged as necessary interlocutors in peace processes, women and girls must be recognized not only as victims, but as "active agents and participants in conflict" and as activists contributing to the survival of their community.

The UN study submitted by the UN Secretary-General pursuant to Security Council Resolution 1325 (2000) gave the international community insights into why women and girls may actively choose to participate in conflict and carry out acts of violence and how they can be coerced into taking up military roles through propaganda, abduction, intimidation and forced recruitment. Women and girls have also provided and continue to provide non-military support to wars through domestic labour, acting as porters, messengers, intelligence officers, disseminating propaganda, becoming combat trainers and encouraging or forcing other children to go to war.

Dyan Mazurana and Susan McKay's study, *Where are the Girls?*, raises our awareness of "the militarization of the lives of girls in fighting forces and the role they play." As it was necessary to separate women from children in order to ensure that women's rights were understood to be human rights, it is now necessary to recognize the realities of girls in armed forces, as the study concludes, in order to recognize gender as a key factor in maintaining fighting forces.

The authors use data gleaned from their research in Northern Uganda, Mozambique and Sierra Leone to show how and where girls are used in fighting forces. They reveal how governments conceal the use of girls in their own militaries, while at the same time pointing to their presence in opposition forces. The denial, concealment and manipulation of information on the use of girls in military forces have serious repercussions on peace-building and reconstruction. Where are the girls, if they are not counted as part of the military when the time comes for disarmament, demobilization and reintegration? How will they return to their communities if they have not begun shedding their fear and guilt? Will anyone be there to heal them? Who will see these girls as both victims and perpetrators? And what kind of society is reconstructed when one is ignored to the benefit of the other?

This groundbreaking study will help policy-makers, program implementers, activists and NGOs to resist the tendency to "pigeonhole" girls in fighting forces. It will help us reflect on who a child is once she has experienced the abuse and torture of the victim and the cruelty and expediency of the perpetrator. It will let us see the importance and value of community healing rituals while remaining vigilant against discriminatory cultural practices.

The importance of the roles played by girls in fighting forces has long been ignored by governments, military, multilateral agencies, community leaders and NGOs. This book forces us to take another look. They are not, and never have been, simply "camp followers"; they are essential to the economy of armed forces, troop morale, their survival and reproductive needs.

It is our hope that this book will lead to the realization that these girls are essential to the future of battered communities, they must be included in disarmament, demobilization and reintegration processes, and they need the love and support of their communities. They were used during war; they want to be useful after it. We also hope that peacemakers will "take into account the gendered physical, psychological, spiritual and social aspects of healing and reintegration" and give girls and women the means to contribute to society. That is the challenge raised by this book.

Jean-Louis Roy
President
Rights & Democracy

Executive Summary

By contributing to what is currently known about girls' distinct experiences in fighting forces, the presentation of findings from our study of girls in fighting forces is intended to assist the Canadian International Development Agency (CIDA), the United Nations, other donors, conflict-affected governments, and local, national and international governmental and non-governmental organizations in developing policies and programs to help protect and empower girls in situations of armed conflict and post-war reconstruction. In addition, this book should alert child protection advocates at all levels to the presence and experiences of girls in fighting forces and facilitate the design of responsive gender-based policy, advocacy and programs.

This book presents findings from a research study entitled "Girls in Militaries, Paramilitaries, Militias, and Armed Opposition Groups" for which we were co-investigators. Our work was funded by CIDA's Child Protection Research Fund and implemented in partnership with Rights & Democracy. The study examined the presence and experiences of girls in fighting forces and groups within the context of three African armed conflicts—Mozambique (1976–1992), Northern Uganda (1986–present) and Sierra Leone (1991–2002). Fieldwork in these countries was conducted between September 2001 and October 2002. In addition to that study, this book includes findings of a parallel study, "Disarmament, Demobilization, and Reintegration: The Experiences and Roles of Girls in Sierra Leone and Northern Uganda," by Dyan Mazurana and Khristopher Carlson, which was funded by the Policy Commission of Women Waging Peace. Fieldwork for this parallel study was conducted between September 2002 and February 2003.

One purpose of this research was to gather and analyze data to better enhance the protection of war-affected children, in particular, girls in fighting forces. Within the context of Northern Uganda, Sierra Leone and Mozambique, girls in the fighting forces have suffered major human rights violations, especially gender-based violence. The rights of these girls are under threat from their own governments, armed opposition forces, and, occasionally, by members of their communities and families. At times, girls are discriminated against by local groups and officials, governments and international bodies that keep secret or are unwilling to recognize their presence, needs and rights during conflict, post-conflict, demobilization and social reintegration.

In Chapter 1, our use of a gender analytic framework reveals that in contemporary and historical wars, armed conflict and militarism intensify sexism through extreme violence perpetrated by boys and men against girls and women, especially sexual violence. We find that girls' experiences within fighting forces are made more severe because of sexism and misogyny. In the aftermath of war, we find that girls and women are usually urged by organizations and community leaders to resume traditional gender roles instead of using the strengths they have developed to make new choices and seek broader opportunities. Based on the realities of their experiences, we offer a definition of "girls in fighting forces" in order to highlight the centrality of girls in these forces, a fact too often overlooked by international, government, military and community officials.

In Chapter 2, we look at the presence, entry and roles of girls in fighting forces from the years 1990 to 2003. We find that girls were part of government, militia, paramilitary and/or armed opposition forces in 55 countries, and were involved in armed conflict in 38 of those countries. In the 55 countries where they are present, girls were recruited by the fighting forces and a number of them made the decision to join. For many, "joining" is a response to violence against themselves or their community, a protection strategy or an opportunity to meet their basic needs. Others enter through being abducted by members of the forces, as occurred in 27 countries. Within the fighting forces, girls carry out a number of diverse roles, including as fighters in 34 countries. Thus, limiting our understanding of the roles they play to those of captive "wives," "sexual slaves" or "camp followers" is inaccurate.

Chapter 3 deals with key dimensions, developments and impacts of armed conflicts in Northern Uganda, Sierra Leone and Mozambique, and our reasons for including each study country.

In Chapter 4, comparative psycho-spiritual, physical and psychological health and sociocultural issues provide a broad thematic overview of the challenges girls face when they attempt to return to their communities after being in a fighting force. Among the key findings is that social reintegration, especially of girl mothers and young women who were girls when they were taken and who return with babies, is particularly difficult and these girls and their children are at high risk. Because relatively few girls go through disarmament and demobilization programs, many spontaneously return to their communities and never receive formal assistance. Their communities may not welcome them because of the stigma attached to rape and giving birth to babies fathered by rebel-captor "husbands." For some returning girls, community rituals—some of which are gender specific—welcome them back and protect the community. An important approach is to work with the entire community to assist it to reintegrate and help these girls heal from trauma. Community approaches are also important in order to address present and past sexual abuse of girls, a subject that is rarely discussed openly in the three study countries. Finally, the psychological and physical health effects reported by girls as a consequence of their experiences in the fighting forces are detailed. Sexually transmitted diseases (STDs) are of particular concern because most girls who return from fighting forces are purportedly infected, yet few are tested or treated. HIV/AIDS represents a major threat to these girls and their children, many of whom will become orphans or die themselves.

Chapter 5 documents and examines girls' and young women's diverse roles in fighting forces in three African countries, Northern Uganda, Sierra Leone and Mozambique, the ways they are recruited into these forces, their under-representation in disarmament, demobilization and reintegration (DDR) programs, and the critical need for schooling and skills training. In Northern Uganda, key findings include documentation of girls' training for and participation in combat. Nearly all captive girls, including those who are pregnant and with small children, are trained as fighters in the rebel Lord's Resistance Army (LRA). Few former captive girls enter the reception or reintegration centres established for those who escape the LRA. Yet the testimony of those who enter reveals that these centres are carrying out essential work in helping to care for the girls and their children, many of whom were born during their captivity. While improvements have been made in the treatment of girls captured and held by the government army, widespread human rights violations continue to occur, including attempted murder, forced recruitment and sexual and physical assault. Finally, these girls and young women are clear about their need to access education and training in skills that will enable them and their children to survive.

In Sierra Leone, key findings include the widespread use of girls by nearly all forces involved in the 1991–2002 war. This includes first-time documentation and analysis of the roles and experiences of girls within government-sponsored militias, "small girl units" and those in charge of rebel fighting compounds. We find that due to a combination of deliberate obstruction, misconceptions about their roles and failed policies, the majority of girls and young women involved in the various fighting forces have been excluded from the government's DDR programs.

As in Northern Uganda, girls and young women in Sierra Leone report that education and skills training would be the most meaningful contribution in assisting their reintegration that local and international agencies could provide.

In Mozambique, girls and young women played many roles within both the government and rebel fighting forces, including as fighters, intelligence officers, spies, porters, medics and slave labour. In both FRELIMO (government) and RENAMO (rebel) fighting forces, they were actively recruited; some willingly joined and some were abducted. Although many Mozambicans were aware of the presence of girls and young women in both forces, international agencies tended to overlook them. This carried through into DDR programs that not only excluded them, but, in some instances, contributed to violations of their human rights, including their remaining captive to men who had abducted them during the war. Others migrated to cities, where they at times sought out others like them to form a community. Most were unable to access valuable skills and education opportunities and today struggle to provide for themselves and their children.

Cross-cutting findings from the three countries reveal governments' manipulation of international outrage over "child soldiers" to discredit armed opposition forces that oppose them, while simultaneously denying or attempting to cover up their own use of girls and boys. We found a pattern of governments pointing to violations of children's rights by armed opposition groups, especially gender-based violations, while failing to address their own forces' violations or to seek remedy for child and youth survivors. The second cross-cutting finding highlights the key information that officials need to use and the action they must take in planning more effective DDR programs for children and youth.

Our conclusion explores the key implications of what it means to really see girls in fighting forces. It details the ways in which this recognition both enables and necessitates a deeper understanding of the types of armed conflicts we are witnessing today and suggests some of the means to address their profound consequences, which are experienced not only by the girls themselves, but by communities, nations and regions.

1. Where are the Girls?

In conducting our study, we used a gender analytic framework, which means we continually thought about how the social construction of gender affects girls and boys, women and men, within the circumstances of armed conflict. We understand gender as socially constructed, with the possibility of limiting or expanding one's options and affecting every aspect of life—for example, opportunities to secure an economic livelihood, access to education and livelihood options, the quality of health care one receives, and excess morbidity and mortality (Mazurana and McKay, 2001).

In reporting our findings, emphasis is given to how girls' experiences within fighting forces are made more severe because of sexism and misogyny. As evidenced in contemporary and historical wars, armed conflict and militarism intensify sexism through extreme violence perpetrated by boys and men against girls and women, especially sexual violence. Within strongly patriarchal societies such as Mozambique, Uganda and Sierra Leone, the countries where the fieldwork was conducted, girls and women are oppressed in countless ways. For example, girls work far more hours than boys, have lower literacy rates than boys and suffer preventable deaths because they lack reproductive health care. Many experience sexual exploitation and abuse in their communities by boys and men. Parents may also be complicit, e.g., pressuring their daughters to exchange sex for goods and money or promoting marriage to men who have raped and abused them.

In all three countries studied, girls in fighting forces carried out traditional gender roles such as cooking, cleaning and serving men, and thus seemingly replicated tasks that women and girls undertake in larger society. Simultaneously, armed conflict and girls' and women's participation in fighting forces sometimes provided opportunities for these girls and women—such as achieving positions of power not previously possible and learning new skills. Thus, war can simultaneously oppress girls and women and expand their possibilities.

In the aftermath of war, girls and women are usually urged to resume traditional gender roles instead of using the strengths they have developed to make new choices and seek broader opportunities. During the post-war period, organizations and influential community members working with girls and women often reinforce their return to traditional structures and patriarchal practices. Therefore, in making recommendations regarding girls who have been in fighting forces or are otherwise war affected, tension exists regarding how advocacy can be used to improve the status of girls and women when gender discrimination still strongly dictates how they live their lives.

Girls and Militarization

Focusing on girls in fighting forces reveals the centrality of the militarization of girls in fuelling and supporting armed conflict. As Mazurana, McKay, Carlson and Kasper (2002) argue,

> By taking the roles of girls in fighting forces and groups as a serious topic of study, we gain a deeper understanding of the factors and underlying stimuli influencing and driving armed conflicts. However familiar it might appear on the surface, there is nothing "natural"—that is, typical or normal, about girls performing tasks for fighting forces or groups. On the contrary, the kinds of tasks and roles girl soldiers are allotted and in some cases forced to undertake are part of a larger planning process deliberately created by those looking to sustain and gain from the armed conflict. Thus, the roles of girl soldiers must be considered as an integral part of the conflict, a window through which we might gain a deeper understanding of the overall conflict itself. What this also means is that demilitarization of these girls needs to be on the forefront of the minds of those planning prevention and reintegration programs (p. 109).

In revealing the militarization of the lives of girls in fighting forces and the roles they play, girls must first and foremost become visible to the international community. Yet little attention has been given to girls' active involvement and distinct experiences.

The question: "Where are the girls?" has only recently been raised in discussions about youth in fighting forces and groups, whether they are combatants or non-combatants. This is due, in large part, to the near-exclusive focus on boys as soldiers and, more recently, on girls and young women as "wives" or "sexual slaves." With the notable exception of data compiled by the International Coalition to Stop the Use of Child Soldiers (Coalition), the majority of reports and international initiatives continue to use the ambiguous term "child soldiers" or "children," almost always meaning boys, and do not identify differential impacts for girls and boys.

Seldom are girls in fighting forces and groups viewed holistically or contextually within specific armed conflicts, geopolitical and cultural contexts, time periods, countries or regions. Very little is known about the distinct physical, emotional and spiritual long-term effects of girls' experiences. Likewise, the varying nature of girls' role expectations and their relationships with men, boys, women and other girls in fighting forces or groups are not well understood. Long-term systematic follow-up, even as recently as a year after fighting has stopped, of what has happened to these girls and their babies and children, is largely absent. Consequently, policies and programs developed to address the needs of these girls are poorly informed or, too often, non-existent.

Throughout this book, we use the term "girls in fighting forces." We do this, in part, in reference to the definition of child soldier found in the *Cape Town Principles* as

> ...any person under 18 years of age who is part of any kind of regular or irregular armed force in any capacity, including but not limited to cooks, porters, messengers, and those accompanying such groups, other than purely as family members. Girls recruited for sexual purposes and forced marriage are included in this definition. It does not, therefore, only refer to a child who is carrying or has carried arms (United Nations Children's Fund [UNICEF], 1997, p. 1).

As explained in the findings of this book, our terminology reflects the reality of girls' experiences and roles in fighting forces, although they are often considered peripheral by government and military officials.

In assessing the advantages and disadvantages of focusing the study on three African countries, we acknowledge that other realities might prevail in different countries and regions. Research in other conflict situations (for example, Keairns, 2002) is needed to improve understanding of the distinct situations of girls in fighting forces in various regions of the world.

Girls and Fighting Forces: International Legal Framework

The principal instruments of international humanitarian law relevant to this study are the protections and guarantees of the four Geneva Conventions of 1949 and their two Additional Protocols of 1977. These protections are granted to all female combatants and civilians without discrimination. Of particular importance to women and girls are the provisions relating to the maintenance and restoration of family ties, and special provisions that require women to be treated with all consideration due to their sex, including reducing vulnerability to sexual violence. Additionally, female prisoners of war, internees and detainees are to be treated with all regard due to their sex and are to be provided with female supervision and accommodation and sanitary facilities separate from males. Added protection is provided for pregnant women and mothers of young children, in particular, regarding access to medical care and physical safety. While the majority of protections under international humanitarian law are limited to situations of inter-state conflict, Protocol II applies to internal conflicts, as does Common Article 3 of the four Geneva Conventions, which prohibits

> ...violence to life and person, in particular murder of all kinds, mutilation, torture, cruel treatment and the taking of hostages, outrages upon personal dignity, in particular humiliating and degrading treatment and the passing of sentences and carrying out of executions without previous judgment carried out by a regularly constituted court, affording judicial guarantees (UN, 2002, p. 35).

International human rights law is of particular significance during non-international armed conflict where international humanitarian law is limited. Human rights obligations include the right to life, freedom from torture and other inhuman and degrading treatment, and freedom from slavery. These rights are found within the *International Convention on the Elimination of All Forms of Racial Discrimination*, the international covenants on civil and political rights and economic, social and cultural rights, the *Convention Against Torture and Other Cruel, Inhuman and Degrading Treatment and Punishment*, and the *Convention on the Rights of the Child*. For example, the *Covenant on Civil and Political Rights* recognizes the rights to life, freedom from arbitrary arrest, slavery and torture. The *Covenant on Economic, Social, and Cultural Rights* recognizes the rights to food, clothing, shelter, health and education. All these instruments apply to women and girls on the basis of non-discrimination.

Further protections are provided by the *Optional Protocol to the Convention on the Rights of the Child* on the sale of children, child prostitution and child pornography and the *Optional Protocol to the Convention on the Rights of the Child* on the involvement of children in armed conflict, which seeks to limit the use of children in armed conflict, including through setting 18 years of age as the minimum age for combat participation. Other key instruments include the *African Charter on the Rights and Welfare of the Child*, the *Rome Statute* of the International Criminal Court, and the International Labour Organization's *Worst Forms of Child Labour Convention 182*.

Whereas humanitarian and human rights protections may exist in international law, their enforcement on the ground in situations of armed conflict is severely limited. The rights of girls in fighting forces are under threat from their own governments, rebel forces, and, at times, members of their communities and families.

Rights-based Approach

In part, a rights-based approach guided the research methods, final analyses and recommendations. With that approach in mind, we focused on gathering data to better enhance the protection of war-affected children, in particular, girls in fighting forces. In addition, a gender analytic framework was used throughout to produce differential analyses of girls and boys, as well as among girls. For example, girl mothers were compared to girls without children, and girls who were commanders' "wives" were compared to those who were "wives" of regular soldiers. Hundreds of in-depth interviews were conducted with girls in fighting forces in the three countries studied to help hone our understanding of their situations and to guide recommendations. The research also focused on documenting and analyzing girls' agency under extremely challenging circumstances and identified girls' coping strategies and community interventions to assist them.

2 Girls in Fighting Forces Worldwide, 1990–2003

To answer in part, "Where are the girls?" we collected global, longitudinal data on the involvement, use and roles of girls in armed forces and armed groups worldwide from 1990–2003. We then used these data to inform comparative analyses and to identify central issues on girls in fighting forces and armed groups.[1]

Few historical accounts exist regarding girls' participation in warfare (see De Pauw, 1998; Edgerton, 2000; Jones, 2000; Mazurana, McKay, Carlson and Kasper, 2002). Yet, both historically and today, girls are present in fighting forces. Between the years 1990–2003, girls were part of fighting forces in 55 countries (Figure 1) Girls were involved in armed conflicts in 38 of these countries (Table 1). In the 38 countries where girls in fighting forces were involved in armed conflicts, the conflicts were internal wars—that is, wars fought among forces within national borders.

Figure 1

Girls in Government Forces, Paramilitary/Militia or Armed Opposition Groups, 1990–2003 [2]

Americas	Middle East	Africa	Europe	Asia
Bolivia G	Iraq G, P/M, O	Angola G, O	Belgium G	Australia G
Canada G	Israel G, O	Burundi G, P/M, O	Bosnia-Herzegovina G, O	Bangladesh G
Colombia G, P/M, O	Lebanon G, P/M, O	Democratic Republic of Congo G, P/M, O	Denmark G, P/M	Cambodia G, P/M, O
Cuba G	Turkey O	Eritrea G, O	Federal Republic of Yugoslavia P/M, O	China G
El Salvador G, P/M, O		Ethiopia G, O	France G, P/M	Democratic Peoples Republic of Korea G, P/M
Guatemala G, P/M, O		Liberia G, O	Ireland G	India P/M, O
Honduras G, O		Libya G	Macedonia O	Indonesia O
Mexico		Mozambique G, P/M, O	Netherlands G	Japan P/M
Nicaragua O		Rwanda G, P/M, O	Norway G, P/M	Myanmar G, O
Peru G, P/M, O		Sierra Leone G, P/M, O	Spain G, P/M	Nepal O
United States G, P/M		Somalia P/M, O	Sweden P/M	Philippines O
		South Africa G, O	United Kingdom G	Sri Lanka O
		Sudan P/M, O		Timor-Leste P/M, O
		Uganda G, O		Uzbekistan O

KEY
Girls under 18 years of age present
- **G** Government forces
- **P/M** Paramilitary/Militia
- **O** Armed opposition groups

---

1 See Appendix 1 for methodology.

2 Data for Figure 1 are drawn from the following sources: Amnesty International [AI], 1997; 1999; Charfi, 1996; Coalition, 2000a; 2000b; 2000c; 2000d; 2000e; 2001; Cock 1993; Cohn & Goodwin, 1994; HRW, 1999, 1998; HRW/Africa/ HRW Children's Rights Project, 1994a; 1994b; 1997; HRW/ Children's Rights Project, 1996; Luciak, 2001; Nordstrom, 1997; PHR, 2000; Radda Barnen, 2000; Refugees International, 2002; Thompson, 1999; UN, 1996; Women's Commission, 2000; World Vision [WV], 1996; Jean-Claude Legrand, interview, July 2001; Celia Petty, interview, March 2000; Jo Becker, Robb Carr, Jean-Claude Legrand and Iain Levine, interview, April 2000; Lieutenant-Commander Cornelis Steenken and Captain Stephen Thompson, interview, June 2000.

Table 1
Girls in Fighting Forces Present in Situations of Armed Conflict, 1990–2003

Africa	Americas	Asia	Europe	Middle East
Angola	Colombia	Burma	Bosnia-Herzegovina	Iraq
Burundi	El Salvador	Cambodia	Federal Republic	Israel
Democratic	Guatemala	India	of Yugoslavia	Lebanon
Republic of Congo	Honduras	Nepal	Macedonia	Palestine
Eritrea	Mexico	Philippines	Northern Ireland	Turkey
Ethiopia	Nicaragua	Sri Lanka	Spain	
Liberia	Peru	Timor-Leste		
Mozambique		Uzbekistan		
Rwanda				
Sierra Leone				
Somalia				
South Africa				
Sudan				
Uganda				

Note: Data for Table 1 are drawn from the same sources listed for Figure 1.

In addition, girls in fighting forces participated in international armed conflicts (fighting between or among nations) in a number of these 38 countries, including Lebanon, Macedonia, Uganda and Sudan.

Girls' Entry into Fighting Forces

Girls enter fighting forces for a variety of reasons (Table 2). In all countries where girls were present (see Figure 1), some of the girls were recruited by fighting forces to join them, with the exceptions of Somalia, Sweden, and possibly Eritrea and Bangladesh.[3] Girls join when they "choose" to become members of a fighting force or group. In all countries where girls are/were present, some of these girls joined the

Table 2
Reasons Girls Enter Armed Forces and Groups, 1990–2003

Recruitment	Taken as orphan	Response to state violence
Join	Born into force	Improve education options
Abduction	"Tax" payment	Improve career options
Compulsory service	Response to local violence	Abuse or problems in home
Protection	Financial gain	Parent, sibling, spouse in forces

Note: Data for Table 2 are drawn from the same sources listed for Figure 1.

---

[3] In Sweden, girls are not actively recruited but may join basic training and weapons training at age 15.

fighting forces, with the possible exceptions of Bangladesh and Somalia (Coalition, 2001). Importantly, the notion of girls freely joining is contested, as is illustrated by the choices girls and boys face currently in the war zones of eastern Democratic Republic of Congo, "join the military, become a street child, or die" (Refugees International, 2002, p. 1).

Abduction occurs when girls are kidnapped or seized by fighting forces or groups and forced to serve in them, as confirmed in 27 countries (see Table 3).

Table 3

Girls Abducted into Armed Forces and Groups, 1990–2003

Africa	Americas	Asia	Europe	Middle East
Angola	Colombia	Burma	Federal Republic of Yugoslavia	Iraq
Burundi	El Salvador	Cambodia	Germany	Turkey
Democratic Republic of Congo	Guatemala	India	Northern Ireland	
	Peru	Indonesia		
Ethiopia		Nepal		
Liberia		Philippines		
Mozambique		Sri Lanka		
Rwanda		Timor-Leste		
Sierra Leone				
Somalia				
Sudan				
Uganda				

Note: Data for Table 3 are drawn from the same sources listed for Figure 1.

"Porous borders, poorly monitored check points, and well-orchestrated schemes to recruit children into fighting forces and groups all allow for the international recruitment and abduction, transport, and trafficking of hundreds of girls world-wide" (Mazurana, McKay, Carlson and Kasper, 2002, p. 107). Although most groups that engage in cross-border abductions to obtain child soldiers are non-state forces, government forces are also involved in cross-border abductions (see Table 4).

Table 4
Girls Abducted and Transported Across International Borders for Participation in Fighting Forces by Country in which Abductions Occur, 1990–2003

Africa	Americas	Asia	Europe	Middle East
Burundi Democratic Republic of Congo Liberia Rwanda Sierra Leone Sudan Uganda	Colombia		Federal Republic of Yugoslavia Germany	Iraq Turkey

Note: Data for Table 4 are drawn from the same sources listed for Figure 1.

Girls' Roles Within Fighting Forces

Girls take on or are forced to assume a number of overlapping roles (see Table 5). Consequently, while it is possible to identify particular roles girls take on, attempts to make clear distinctions among them are often inaccurate, for example, fighters vs. "wives" or cooks vs. spies. Thus, it is necessary to view girls in fighting

Table 5
Roles and Activities Assumed by Girls in Fighting Forces, 1990–2003

Combat soldiers	Porters	Spies
Trainers for combat	Looting	Informants
Slave labour	Suicide/bombing missions	Messengers
Sexual slave	Mine sweeps	Intelligence officers
Gather, prepare, cook food	Child care and rearing	Communications

Note: Data for Table 5 are drawn from the same sources listed for Figure 1.

forces within the specific context of the armed force or group, as well as the larger political, social, cultural and economic context of the conflict itself.

Girls have been active as fighters within armed conflict (see Table 6), and girls continue to be present in fighting forces currently engaged in armed conflict (see Table 7).

Table 6

Girls Serving as Fighters in Armed Conflict, 1990–2003

Africa	Americas	Asia	Europe	Middle East
Burundi	Colombia	Burma	Bosnia-Herzegovina	Iraq
Democratic	El Salvador	Cambodia	Federal Republic	Israel
Republic of Congo	Guatemala	India	of Yugoslavia	Lebanon
Eritrea	Honduras	Nepal	Macedonia	Palestine
Ethiopia	Mexico	Philippines	Northern Ireland	Turkey
Liberia	Nicaragua	Sri Lanka	Spain	
Mozambique	Peru	Timor-Leste		
Rwanda				
Sierra Leone				
Sudan				
Uganda				

Note: Data for Table 6 are drawn from the same sources listed for Figure 1.

Table 7

Girls in Fighting Forces Present in Countries Experiencing Armed Conflict as of November 2003

Africa	Americas	Asia	Europe	Middle East
Angola*	Colombia	Burma	Spain	Israel
Burundi		India		Lebanon
Democratic		Nepal		Palestine
Republic of Congo		Philippines		
Liberia		Sri Lanka		
Somalia				
Sudan				
Uganda				

Note: Data for Table 7 are drawn from the same sources listed for Figure 1.
*Indicates forces currently in ceasefire or large-scale disarmament.

Girls are, in some contexts, systematically forced to provide sexual services to males within the fighting forces (see Table 8), and sexual violence against girls is a common experience. In most cases of abducted girls, their bodies and their domestic and sexual labour are commodities that are coveted, traded, and, at times, fought over.

Table 8
Girls in Fighting Forces Forced to Provide Sexual Services, 1990–2003

Africa ○	Americas	Asia	Europe	Middle East
Angola	Colombia	Burma	Bosnia-Herzegovina	
Burundi	Honduras	Cambodia	Kosovo (Yugoslavia)	
Democratic Republic of Congo	Peru	India		
Liberia		Indonesia		
Mozambique		Timor-Leste		
Rwanda				
Sierra Leone				
Sudan				
Uganda				

Note: Data for Table 8 are drawn from the same sources listed for Figure 1.

While these tables provide some insight into the scope of girls' participation and roles, much more research is needed to learn about girls' experiences and circumstances. However, one conclusion can be drawn: the UN, governments, NGOs and INGOs must assume the presence of girls in fighting forces in most armed conflicts and plan policies and programs that are designed to address their experiences, needs and rights, and that are gender sensitive.

3 War in Northern Uganda, Sierra Leone and Mozambique: Background and Overview

Our study focused on collecting in-depth data on three countries in Africa (refer to Appendix 1 for a complete discussion of data collection, management and analysis). In this section, we offer an overview of key dimensions, developments and impacts of armed conflicts in Northern Uganda, Sierra Leone and Mozambique, followed by our rationale for including each study country.

We selected countries that represented several key dimensions:
1. presence of children and youth, including girls, within at least one of the fighting forces;
2. countries with children and youth in fighting forces still experiencing conflict and those where the armed conflict had lessened or ceased;
3. countries where either little international awareness existed regarding the presence of girls or where greater awareness of such girls existed;
4. countries with girls in fighting forces where regional and UN peacekeeping forces operated and assisted the government in design and implementation of official disarmament, demobilization and reintegration (DDR) programs and those where national forces were responsible for official DDR programs, and;
5. countries where children and youth, including girls, were currently passing through UN or national DDR programs and countries where the reintegration programs occurred several years ago to allow for retrospection. Based on these criteria, we chose to conduct in-depth fieldwork regarding the conflicts in Northern Uganda (1986–present), Sierra Leone (1991–2002) and Mozambique (1976–1992).[4]

---

4 While fighting continued in some regions until 1994, the year multi-party elections were held, the war officially ended in 1992 with the signing of peace accords in Rome.

Armed Conflict in Northern Uganda, 1986 to the Present

The ongoing armed conflict in Northern Uganda began in 1986 with the coming to power of the National Resistance Movement, the subsequent flight of opposition fighters into Northern Uganda and Southern Sudan and their pursuit by government forces, leading to growing unrest in that region. In 1987, in Northern Uganda, Joseph Kony (pronounced "Kohn") started what is now known as the rebel Lord's Resistance Army (LRA) (Finnstrom, 2001; Human Rights Watch (HRW)/Africa and HRW/ Children's Rights Project, 1997). The war intensified between the LRA and the government Ugandan People's Defence Force (UPDF) during 1993 and 1994 when the government of Sudan offered the LRA sanctuary, military bases and supplies within its southern border. This enabled the LRA to increase its abductions, particularly of girls and young women, and to take its new captives to bases in Sudan for training, as well as to establish bases where the slave labour of captive girls and young women helped support the fighting force. The war in Northern Uganda increasingly served as an internal war and a proxy war for both Uganda and Sudan (Rone, 1998) as, up until at least 2002, the two countries funded, armed, supplied and trained the others' rebel forces.

The war within Northern Uganda and Southern Sudan has been a war against the civilian populations inhabiting this region. It is marked by extreme brutality and includes sexual abuse, sexual, physical and mental torture, unlawful arrest and detention, disfigurement and mutilation, forced cannibalism and a wide array of threats (Isis-WICCE, 2001a, 2001b). Abductions into the rebel forces are a central part of the conflict. Because the LRA cannot attract many fighters into its ranks, it fills them primarily with abducted boys and girls. The practice of abduction is particularly devastating to the family structure and future of the north: UNICEF estimates that 80 percent of the LRA is comprised of abducted adolescents who are forced to attack their own families, neighbours, and villages (Women's Commission, 2001); see also Amnesty International (AI), 1997; HRW/Africa and HRW/Children's Rights Project, 1997). Both Northern Ugandan and Southern Sudanese girls and boys are abducted. Although children between the ages of 12 and 16 make up the majority of those abducted, civilians of all ages have been abducted, usually with the recent abductees forced to carry out actions against family members or neighbours or face summary death by torture and mutilation. The purpose of such violence is twofold, to destroy the link between the captive and her or his family and community, and to initiate the abductee into the rebel force.

The Ugandan government stationed the Fourth Division of the government UPDF in Gulu District to counter the attacks by the LRA and provide security to the people who increasingly moved into internally-displaced persons' (IDP) camps (Isis-WICCE, 2001a, 2001b; Women's Commission, 2001). A number of grassroots groups, including groups of parents, religious and traditional leaders and national and international NGOs have organized to attempt to bring peace to the region and assist the war-affected population. It was largely due to pressure from these groups that the government passed an Amnesty Law. Local groups made up of mothers and fathers who have lost their children have also played a significant role in trying to bring the LRA and the government to the peace table, most notably in July and August of 2002, and February of 2003, and in securing the release of some children from the LRA (HRW, March and July 2003; Dr. Frank Olyet interview, February 14, 2003).

In early 2002, improved bilateral relations between the Sudanese and Ugandan governments led to Sudan granting Uganda military access to its southern borders to pursue the LRA. Launched in March 2002 with 10,000 Ugandan troops, "Operation Iron Fist" forced the LRA out of Southern Sudan and into Northern Uganda. The results have been devastating for civilian populations in both Northern Uganda and Southern Sudan, including thousands of new abductions by the LRA, abandonment of entire sub-counties to avoid fighting, the displacement of an additional 400,000 people, increased child recruitment by the UPDF, and the forced removal of people from their lands into government "protected villages." The war has now reached the most destructive level since it began, with attacks and abductions occurring on a daily basis, the re-emergence of the LRA back into Southern Sudan, and the recent establishment of semi-permanent rebel bases in Northern Uganda. A number of ceasefires, many brokered by local and religious leaders, have been repeatedly broken by both the LRA and the Ugandan government and fighting and insecurity continue (HRW, March and July 2003).

Rationale for Selection: Northern Uganda was selected for inclusion in the study because of the widespread abduction and use of child captives by the rebel LRA forces in the North. Estimates place 70 to 80 percent of the LRA as child combatants, with girls making up approximately 30 percent of these forces. Additionally, a number of UN agencies and international and local NGOs are working with these children and their communities, enabling greater access for the researchers. Among these groups, there is widespread awareness of the presence of girls within the forces. As no UN or regional peacekeeping force is present, disarmament and demobilization of former captives and fighters is carried out by the government UPDF forces working in conjunction with UN humanitarian bodies, NGOs and community leaders, which in turn work on the reintegration of the returnees.

Armed Conflict in Sierra Leone (1991–2002)

In March 1991, Revolutionary United Front (RUF) rebels, backed by Charles Taylor's forces of the National Patriotic Front of Liberia (NPFL), invaded Sierra Leone from Liberia and occupied the eastern regions of the country, securing lucrative diamond reserves. The war involved Liberia, Guinea and Côte d'Ivoire. In exchange for weapons, drugs and supplies, the RUF leadership smuggled Sierra Leonean diamonds back into Liberia for sale on the international market, generating millions of dollars annually. However, the RUF movement failed to attract widespread local support; consequently, forced conscription and abduction of both boys and girls were widely carried out. Women and girls interviewed by Physicians for Human Rights (PHR) reported that most of the abuse they suffered was at the hands of the RUF (PHR, 2002).

As government revenues fell from the loss of mineral sales, so too did the salaries and the resolve of the Sierra Leone Army (SLA). During the war, SLA soldiers committed gross human rights violations, including rape, mutilation, looting, property destruction and murder. By the mid-1990s, citizens directly associated the problem of the war with the army itself. With the rebellion spreading virtually unchecked in the South and East, villagers organized militias to supplement or replace the efforts of the army. The local militias became known as Civil Defence Forces (CDFs) (Bangura, 2000; Richards, 2001).

Some SLA soldiers joined the RUF to become part of the new rebel Armed Forces Revolutionary Council (AFRC). In 1997, the AFRC overthrew President Kabbah's regime. Shortly thereafter, the RUF was invited to join the new regime. Support for the AFRC came from professionals, civil servants, politicians and other members of the socio-economic elite who felt alienated from the Kabbah government (Bangura, 2000). The signing of the *Lomé Peace Accord* officially ended the war in 1999 (though fighting and unrest continued into 2002) and set the parameters for the DDR program. In October 1999, UN Assistance Mission to Sierra Leone (UNAMSIL) troops deployed to Sierra Leone to support the implementation of the *Lomé Peace Accord* and assist in the DDR process (Francis, 2000). The war was officially declared over in January 2002.

During the war, nearly a quarter of the population was internally displaced, while hundreds of thousands became refugees. Hundreds of hospitals and schools and tens of thousands of homes were destroyed. With a lack of basic health care services, failing schools, and the widespread destruction of infrastructure, the population grew increasingly vulnerable to abuse, including abduction, by nearly all forces. Sierra Leone's countryside became militarized, with the presence of international forces, widespread proliferation of small arms, and general suspicion towards one's neighbours, especially in areas protected by local militias. Women and girls reported atrocities, committed by all fighting forces during the war (AI, 2001; HRW, 1998; PHR, 2002).

In the post-conflict context, two important avenues of justice for the people of Sierra Leone are the Truth and Reconciliation Commission (TRC) and the Special Court for Sierra Leone. The TRC is an independent organization created by the *Lomé Accords*, mandated to create an impartial historical record of the violations of humanitarian law and human rights related to the 1991–2002 armed conflict, address impunity, respond to victims, and promote healing and reconciliation.[5] The Special Court was created by the UN and Sierra Leone government in 2000 and has jurisdiction over crimes against humanity, war crimes and other serious violations of international humanitarian law and state law committed within the territory of Sierra Leone during the conflict. Both the statutes of the TRC and the Special Court reflect a number of key developments regarding the use of children as combatants and the rights of women and girls under international standards (UN, 2002).

Rationale for Selection: Sierra Leone's 1991–2001 conflict was selected because of the widespread use of child soldiers by all fighting forces (except the Economic Community of West African States Monitoring Group [ECOMOG] and UN peacekeeping missions). Extensive international awareness existed about abduction of children, especially of girls, and forcible recruitment of boys and girls by the rebel forces. Again, a number of UN agencies and INGOs knew of the presence of child soldiers and developed programs to address these populations. The country also hosted large regional ECOMOG and UN peacekeeping missions (UNAMSIL). DDR was carried out by the government, in conjunction with the UN peacekeeping missions, UN agencies, and international and national NGOs.

Armed Conflict in Mozambique (1976–1992)

The war between the government Frente de Libertação Nacional (FRELIMO) forces and the counter-insurgency forces of Resistencia Nacional de Moçambique (RENAMO) began after Mozambique won its war of independence from Portugal in 1974. RENAMO was initially created and backed by the Rhodesian government and later the apartheid government of South Africa. However, FRELIMO's policies of disempowering local and traditional leaders, as well as land reform and ethnic elitism, resulted in many people joining RENAMO as the conflict progressed. FRELIMO was supported by the Eastern socialist bloc and therefore suffered economically and politically during the Cold War (Chingono, 1996; HRW/Africa Watch, 1992).

---

5 Information regarding the Sierra Leone TRC can be found at www.sierra-leone.org/trc-documents.html.

The conflict resulted in almost one million dead, 45 percent of whom were children. One-and-a-half million people fled the country as refugees, and another three million became internally displaced. The war devastated the infrastructure, with schools and medical facilities systematically targeted by RENAMO. Both sides recruited and gang-pressed girls and boys into their forces throughout the conflict. These children were used as combatants, spies, slaves, "wives," intelligence agents and porters. Families were torn apart and physical and sexual violence, including murder, amputation, rape, forced cannibalism and torture, were widespread (HRW/Africa Watch, 1992; Vines, 1991).

With the official end of the war in 1992, UN Operations in Mozambique (ONUMOZ) worked with the FRELIMO government to carry out DDR; 27 percent of those demobilized were under 18 years of age. The war left a legacy of over two million anti-personnel mines, devastated educational and health systems, stockpiles of weapons, and a generation of children and adults severely affected by the economic, political, environmental, social, psychological and physical health effects of the war (Efraime and Errante, nd; Thompson, 1999; Vines, 1991).

Rationale for Selection: Mozambique during the 1976–1992 war was selected because it was the first time that the use of child soldiers was raised internationally, in this case by the FRELIMO government publicly displaying boy soldiers from rebel RENAMO forces. One response by the international community was the development of specific programs for child soldiers; only boys passed through the programs. During the Mozambique conflict, child soldiers became such a "hot issue" that neither the government nor RENAMO wanted to admit using them; thus alternative programs were developed in order to gain the release of the children. Mozambique also presented an opportunity to document and assess the experiences of young women who were in the fighting forces. For the most part, the presence of women in the fighting forces was grudgingly acknowledged by internationals, but the use of girls was widely denied or dismissed as infrequent. No specific post-conflict programs were developed for girls, and gender considerations in children's programs were nearly nonexistent. Girls received few, if any, benefits and were struggling for survival years later. Between 1992 and 1994, the UN worked with the government to carry out an official DDR process; both the larger UN peacekeeping mission and DDR were deemed successful by the UN and a number of international observers.

4. Comparative Findings of Psycho-spiritual, Physical and Psychological Health, and Sociocultural Issues

To survive war is to personally and collectively deal with its horrific aftermath—the trauma to the body, psyche and soul, the devastation of communities and the effects on quality of life. The challenge for communities is to come to terms with what has happened and develop a renewed sense of present and future possibilities, and to be able to heal as a collective. Yet, these are "soft effects" because they are about people rather than institutions and their importance easily is overlooked. Thinking about communities is seldom a priority of international funding agencies and policy makers, whose efforts during the post-war period are typically directed towards reconstructing the physical, political, educational and economic infrastructures. Although trickle-down effects may be envisioned as part of the reconstruction process, in actuality, communities seldom benefit directly and, for the most part, must rely on their own resources.

Increasingly, international and national NGOs, bolstered by UN agencies such as UNICEF, have directed much of their work towards working with communities to develop psychosocial programs that support healing and build upon community strengths and resiliency. Even within these initiatives, until very recently, girls have not been thought about because there has been a lack of recognition of their participation in fighting forces and the suffering they experienced. This inherent gender discrimination has made them invisible within demobilization and reintegration programs. To compound girls' difficulties, they often face gender discrimination in their communities and are not easily accepted back—especially if they bring children born of forced sex. Communities need focused assistance to develop their capacities to protect and help these girls. Policy makers must prioritize initiatives that assist communities to be key actors in supporting girls' spiritual and psychological healing and responding to their needs.

The findings in this section,[6] authored by co-investigator of the CIDA/Rights & Democracy study, Susan McKay, focus upon physical and psycho-spiritual health issues of girls associated with fighting forces in Northern Uganda, Sierra Leone and Mozambique. Key issues for these girls are delineated, substantiated with study data and linked with key studies and expert reports. Recommendations for policy and programmatic actions are given for each finding.

---

6 Methodology is discussed in Appendix 1.

Community-based Reintegration Programs
FINDING:
Community-based reintegration programs are insufficiently sensitive to the needs of returning girls.

Spontaneous (self, continuous, "going straight home") reintegration of girls is by far the most common way girls return from fighting forces and is largely a hidden process, whereby girls are assimilated directly back into their communities. In Northern Uganda, spontaneous reintegration is the prevalent pattern for returning girls. This same pattern occurred in Sierra Leone and Mozambique, with girls infrequently participating in formal DDR processes. The result is that large numbers of returned girls in each of the three countries studied did or do not have focused DDR or social reintegration assistance to provide physical, material and psychosocial help.

Research indicates that returnee children may not do as well without these forms of assistance. A field study was conducted with a subject pool of 567 Northern Ugandan children from the Gulu, Kitgum and Pader districts (412 male and 155 female). Of these children, 73.5 percent had been abducted, whereas 26.5 percent (N=150)[7] lived in the same districts but were never abducted. The researchers concluded that children who went straight home (59 girls and 96 boys) and did not pass through any reception and/or rehabilitation centres before returning to their families were less confident and more anxious, depressed and hostile than children who went through a program. Additionally, research assistants for this study observed that children who went straight home appeared to be the least well adjusted of the former abductees (MacMullin and Loughry, 2002). Noteworthy is that, of the 262 children who went through one of two rehabilitation centres (Kitgum Concerned Women's Association (KICWA) in Kitgum or World Vision (WV) in Gulu City), 41 (15.6 percent) girls who had been abducted and 221 (84.4 percent) boys who had been abducted participated in formal programs of rehabilitation and reintegration. These gender-skewed participation data point to the possibility that girls in Northern Uganda may more frequently go straight home than boys and therefore are less likely to benefit from programs for returning children.

Likewise, at the end of the war in Mozambique, although girls constituted 40 percent of the minors initially documented at the RENAMO bases, "the great absence in many programmes are [were] the girls" (Draisma and Mucache, 1997, p. 13). Reports indicated that [some] "girls who wished to be reunited with their family were forced to stay with their partner [RENAMO 'husband'] or leave with him to his home"

---

7 "N" indicates numbers of interviews.

even though traditional marriage (Lobolo) had not taken place (Draisma and Mucache, 1997). Other reports indicated that some girls and women were abandoned by their RENAMO "husbands" during demobilization (Draisma and Mucache, 1997).

In DDR programs in Sierra Leone, few girls participated; many went straight back to their communities or to family members. Similarly, a case study of DDR in Sierra Leone (UNICEF, unpublished manuscript) reported that girls who returned to their communities tended to bypass formal systems and return anonymously. While this secrecy protected them, it also concealed their need for support. Susan Shepler, a Sierra Leonean scholar who lived in a Sierra Leonean village as a Peace Corps volunteer and later conducted doctoral research for 18 months in interim care centres in Freetown, noted that for returning girls in Sierra Leone,

> ...a lot of their strategy is secrecy. They slink back home and don't want anyone to know what happened to them. To a much greater extent than boys. So it is easier to find the boys because they go through formal programs and are more open about their situation. Girls just went home, without letting anyone know and are hiding their situation... they look at various strategies for reintegration and the best strategy for them is just to go back to their village and downplay what happened to them. I think they initially go back to their own family and if that works out, they stay there. But often it doesn't work out, and they go someplace else. Sometimes that means the city, sometimes going back with a former commander (Susan Shepler interview, April 5, 2002).

Whether they will be welcomed upon return, especially if they have children born of rebel captor-fathers, is a source of concern for girls. Consistent with our study findings and estimates of girls' reintegration rates, we concluded that few girls go through formal programs intended to demobilize, rehabilitate and reintegrate children who have been in with fighting forces. Instead they return directly to their communities.

How girls fare when they return: The majority of girls in our study did not serve as primary combatants. When they returned, often with the stigma of having been a "wife" of a rebel captor-"husband" or the mother of a baby fathered by a rebel, they faced specific reintegration challenges. The success of girls' reintegration is tied to a number of variables. These include the pattern of how she was taken into a fighting force, the length of time she was in the force, the military role she played, and how she returned. As an example, a cohort of girls abducted and who return to the community together will usually be viewed more favourably than girls who return unaccompanied or remain in a force for an extended period and return with one or more children. Shepler researched how former child soldiers in Sierra Leone negotiated their way through interim care centres and strategies they used. Shepler thinks that when children in Sierra Leone are gone a short time, it is easier for communities to believe they were held against their will,

> They come back and say "it wasn't my fault, I was abducted, I was on drugs" and that helps them get into the community… there is a sense that the ones gone longer are more hardened… And also, who knows what happened in those years? There is more time to imagine what kind of atrocities they might have committed (Susan Shepler interview, April 5, 2002).

Adjustment difficulties may accelerate when returnees are abducted as children and subsequently spend years in a fighting force where they learn behaviours that helped them survive in the bush but which can hinder their reintegration. A study of 42 former Mozambican boy soldiers, aged 6 to 16 years, concluded that "the length of time spent in a RENAMO base camp was more strongly associated with later continued anti-social and violent or aggressive behaviour than was the degree of personal involvement in violence; thus, boys who spent one or two years with RENAMO had shifted self identities to be 'as one with their captors'" (Boothby as cited in Arnston and Boothby, 2002, p. 3). MacMullin and Loughry (2002) concluded in their study of children in Northern Uganda that "time in captivity has a strong influence on the level of anxiety, pro-social behaviour and hostility" (p. 11).

In our three study countries, girls were reported to display difficult behaviour when they spent extended time in fighting forces. Anti-social behaviour—such as being aggressive, quarrelsome, using abusive language, killing and eating others' animals, abusing drugs and smoking—violated gender norms and affected their ability to readjust to their community and the community's response to them. As noted by Shepler, "it was easier [in Sierra Leone] for the villages to accept troublesome boys because 'boys will be boys.' Troublesome girls are much harder to reintegrate. A key to successful reintegration is 'being like everybody else,' and troublesome behaviour contravenes this goal" (Susan Shepler interview, April 5, 2002).

Because of norms and social circumstances, former female combatants may not want to be recognized as such because they will not be well received; therefore they can, to varying degrees, avoid stigma by hiding their pasts and making the best of the situation rather than seeking help (Barth 2002). Stavrou, Stewart and Stavrou (2000), in a 1999 study conducted in Northern Uganda, observed that for escaping women or girls who come back home, "the perception that they were willing wives of the rebel commanders makes them untouchables—as if they have been used up. They suffer shame and humiliation from other children and adults who taunt and tease them" (p. 16). Angulo (2000) also studied abducted children in Northern Uganda and concluded that whereas both boys and girls found it hard to settle and interact in communities, reintegrating was harder for girls because they faced negative attitudes and perceptions due to their forced loss of virginity (the term used in Northern Uganda is "defilement" whereas in Sierra Leone, girls say they were "devirginalized"). In Sierra Leone, many girls and young women endured stigmatization and being branded as "rebels" when they returned to their communities from the RUF; few received counselling and support negotiating their "bush marriages" or recovering from sexual or other violence (Women's Commission, 2002).

A workshop report on the use of child soldiers in the African Great Lakes region also found that girls face greater stigmatization upon reintegration than boys and that child mothers need more support because this cohort faces higher levels of community rejection (Coalition, 2002). Shepler questioned why few reintegration programs exist for girls and why these programs don't do well serving this population: "The answer can be found by understanding the set of cultural possibilities for girls" (Susan Shepler interview, April 5, 2002). Shepler's research indicates "that in many cases it is easier for a boy to be accepted after amputating the hands of villagers than it is for a girl to be accepted after being the victim of rape" (Shepler, 2002, pp 9-10).

The degree of preparation of the girl and her family for reunification, especially after long separations and when girls return with children, is a critical factor in successful reintegration. Girls who spontaneously find their way home are at risk because they often do not receive primary physical and psychosocial health care. Issues of special concern for girls' reintegration include stigma, threats, physical abuse, and sexual violence committed by boys and men in the community. Also, girls may return to their communities but not stay because they experience reintegration difficulties, lack opportunities, or they themselves have changed so profoundly as a result of their association with fighting forces that they no longer fit into the community. Among variables that can affect whether they remain within the community are their age when they return, whether the community infrastructure is intact and their parents and siblings still live there, if they are able to meet their basic minimum material needs, whether they can live free of abuse by family and community members, and safety within the community.

Recovery: A key to recovery is the establishment of a trusting relationship with a caring adult. Living with parents may be a critical factor in children's recovery. For example, MacMullin and Loughry (2000) found children in Northern Uganda to be less depressed when they lived with their parents, as compared to guardians, after they escaped the LRA.

"It is to parents and communities that children, whether boys, girls, or girls with babies will return" (UNICEF Eastern and Southern Africa Regional Office, 2001, p. 48). Abubacar Sultan, UNICEF Child Protection Officer in Angola, observed that "the truth is that the child's reintegration occurs more rapidly and with less stigma or discrimination as relatives and communities become responsible for them right at the beginning" of demobilization (Abubacar Sultan, personal communication, January 9, 2003). Thus, the psychosocial intervention goal is "to create a more positive social reality for the child through broader assistance efforts that help to support or to re-establish the child's primary relationships to parents, families, communities, and, in some cases, larger ethnic groups" (Arntson and Boothby, 2002, p. 1).

Program planning: The principles of action of reintegration programmes "must be based on the needs of the children and those of their families and communities" and "must promote the best interest of the child" (Legrand, 1999, p. 27). Thompson (1999) observed how, in contrast to Western cultures where approaches to injustice are individualistic, in post-war Mozambique, responsibility is a social concern. Further, community capacity to care for and protect children must be strengthened so that communities are assisted in preparing for the return of its children and can support them as they regain normal lives. Yet, if communities are to assume this responsibility, they must be supported by programs that enable them to effectively respond to the needs of returning children. McConnan and Uppard asserted that,

> A priority should be to give advice and support to parents or other carers since they themselves can do much to help their own children. Agencies should seek to encourage a sense of community responsibility for the children, emphasizing their wider rights, while at the same time considering the needs of other children in the community (McConnan and Uppard, 2001 p. 171).

An example in Sierra Leone was a group of communities that, with the help of an INGO, identified a large cohort of sexually abused girls without delineating those who were associated with fighting forces and those who were war-affected. Of these girls, a subset was selected by the community to receive assistance. A second example is a program for girls with babies under two years old that was developed for both abducted girls with babies and high-risk war-affected girls with babies. Other examples of initiatives are drop-in centres for girls and day care centres for single mothers.

Community upheaval: Communities continue to change and reformulate themselves when they are in the midst of violent conflict and many no longer exist. As observed by Veale and Stavrou in Northern Uganda, "There is no community, in terms of what was... In essence the conflict has broken down the very fabric of Acholi society," (Veale and Stavrou, 2002, p. 28). Both Barth (2002), who studied female fighters in Eritrea, and Veale and Stavrou, who studied former LRA abductees (2002), asked the question: "Reintegration into what?" They pointed out that "community reintegration implies a removal from a community of origin and then a physical and psychological reinsertion back into that social relational and psychological space" (Veale and Stavrou, 2002, p. 28). This may be impossible when the community no longer exists or is disjointed, displaced, reconfigured, or otherwise dissimilar to what it was before they left.

Girls may return but not stay in their former communities because they have experienced too many identity and personal changes or face too many reintegration barriers, especially if they have been gone an extended time. Often they are not able to take care of themselves and their children within their communities, or their families may refuse to let them return (Barth, 2002). Legrand (1999) and Veale (2003) noted that female ex-combatants from some conflicts have trouble reintegrating into traditional communities after experiencing independent and egalitarian lives in the military. When they return, these girls and women may experience gender role discontinuity that challenges them at all levels of their daily lives—a finding that emerged from Veale's study of 11 former Tigrean women ex-fighters. Because they changed as a result of their experiences, they challenge traditional roles that they cannot accept (Veale, 2003), hence the notion of "troublesome girls" who do not adhere to normal gender roles. In our study, egalitarian relationships between sexes in fighting forces were not evident; instead, girls and women were subjected to oppression, gender-specific violence, abusive and violent relationships, with rare opportunities to exercise autonomy.

Girls who have been associated with fighting forces consistently experience "second-rate" reintegration, when compared with boys. In consideration of this study finding, the following recommendations are offered:

POLICY RECOMMENDATIONS
Governments, the United Nations, multilateral agencies and INGOs should

> Fund and conduct comparative gender studies to document community-based program responses and outcomes for reintegrating children and longitudinal research to improve understanding of the implications of "second-rate" reintegration, in which girls experience strong discrimination. A critical question to ask is, "What factors make it possible for girls to reintegrate into their communities and what prevents their reintegration?"

> Mainstream gender training of child protection workers as one step towards increasing gender awareness in policy and program development. Include curricula about women's and children's rights. Despite knowledge about the effects of sexist behaviour and gender discrimination, from international to grassroots levels, the mainstreaming of gender perspectives remains low.

> Work in interdisciplinary ways with child protection agencies, maternal and child health programs, human rights groups, and local and national women leaders and women's peacebuilding networks to improve the situation of girls and to integrate gender-appropriate approaches to child protection in all humanitarian work (food assistance, security, shelter, health). Examples of effective programs are Rebuilding Hope in Mozambique, FAWE (Forum of African Women's Educationalists) in Sierra Leone, Concerned Parents Association (CPA) in Northern Uganda, Christian Children's Fund (CCF) in Sierra Leone, International Rescue Committee (IRC) in Sierra Leone and Northern Uganda, Save the Children (SC) and World Vision (WV) in Northern Uganda, and Canadian Physicians for Aid and Relief (CPAR) in Northern Uganda.

> Explain and support "affirmative action" or "positive discrimination" as one criterion to ensuring the equitable treatment of girls and boys that is necessary in order to meet obligations under international human rights law and to bolster post-conflict development.

PROGRAM RECOMMENDATIONS
Governments, the United Nations, multilateral agencies and INGOs should

> Learn the context in which girls reintegrate, because girls have diverse reintegration experiences. Girls' own perceptions of their situations must serve as a basis for needs assessment during post-conflict reintegration. They should be involved in meaningful ways in planning, implementing, and evaluating programs of assistance for themselves.

> Work with communities, families and girls themselves to assure that returning girls are not segregated or marginalized in social reintegration programs, because such approaches can further "brand" them, especially if they receive enhanced assistance. A better approach is for war-affected communities to participate, through dialogue, in identifying girls who most need assistance.

> Explore programmatic approaches that ensure attention to those who were unjustly left out of the DDR process. This may provide critical assistance for self-reintegrating girls who are neglected in terms of DDR benefits, psychosocial counselling, health care, and skills training. Plan and develop general programming for girls, in consultation with them, which takes into account their holistic needs in achieving successful reintegration.

> Prioritize specific and practical assistance for disabled (for example, blind, hearing impaired, or amputee), separated and orphaned girls. These girls are at high risk in their communities and have greater difficulty in fulfilling normal gender roles and securing resources for survival.

> Form NGO partnerships with grassroots individuals and groups already working with girls, such as teachers, traditional leaders, religious leaders, parents and women elders because of their potential to work with girls over time. Aims should include capacity building, partnership and empowerment.

> When appropriate, support short-term separation of girls from their communities after they leave fighting forces—such as the WV and GUSCO rehabilitation centres in Northern Uganda and the Conforti Center for pregnant girls and mothers in Sierra Leone. Interim care centres for returning children can play an important part in rehabilitation and reintegration, but must be conceived and operated as part of a total program that also has a strong community-based component, as well as advocacy.

Mediation, Problem Solving and Community Dialogue to Help Reintegrating Girls

FINDING:

Results-based outcomes that start from problem-solving strategies including conflict resolution, dialogue and mediation processes, rather than "sensitization," should be used to help meet the needs of returning girls.

In the context of demobilization and reintegration processes, the term "sensitization" usually means that NGOs and grassroots groups prepare families and communities for children's return by helping them change their awareness and educating them about children's rights. In addition, they prepare children for what they might expect when they return to those communities. This emphasis of "sensitization" upon awareness and principles of child rights does not necessarily translate into behaviour change and making children's rights a reality within the community.

"Sensitization," whatever its specifics and interpretation, is widely perceived as an important activity prior to girls' (and boys') reintegration. Although "sensitization" of communities was discussed in both Sierra Leone and Uganda, we heard "sensitization talk" far more frequently in Sierra Leone, because it reflects a major objective of national and international rights-based organizations that work with children and youth. NGO workers, in particular, discussed the return of girls and girls with children with their "sensitizing" communities. "Sensitization" was thought necessary because community animosity existed towards these children and families said they no longer wanted them.

An important component of most "sensitization" messages is that children were forced or drugged (thereby violating their rights) and were not responsible for what they did. Usually after several visits to the family and community, the family and community are evaluated as "sensitized" (aware) and ready for the child's return. "Sensitization talk" also extends to issues of sexually abused girls and girl mothers with their babies and/or children. No standard definition exists about what "sensitization" entails nor do measures exist to evaluate whether behaviour change has occurred. Further, "sensitization" messages may be scripted top down rather than developed collaboratively with communities.

"Sensitization" can be done poorly. As observed by Michael Wessells of the Christian Children's Fund, United States,

> Too often the problem is that sensitization is not coupled with problem solving; communities may be aware that particular problems may arise, but they have no strategies for addressing them. Thus the follow-up should be more than a check that the messages have 'taken'—the key task is to make sure groups in the community can help create and enable an environment for safe, equal return and reintegration and to assist in the provision of material resources that are critical to achieving this goal (Michael Wessells, personal communication, January 7, 2003).

Wessells noted that how "sensitization" is carried out becomes critical since some groups accomplish "sensitization" by "driving up in white cars and getting out with their CRC *[Convention on the Rights of the Child]* lists," beginning a process of imposition. Due to the vagaries associated with the word "sensitization" and its ubiquitous and often non-specific use, some groups have stopped using the term because it can incorporate any topic, such as education about HIV/AIDS or the Truth and Reconciliation Commission in Sierra Leone.

Elizabeth Jareg of Save the Children, Norway, believes that the term "sensitization" fails to convey the enormous amount of work spent in discussions with communities (Elizabeth Jareg, personal communication, January 8, 2003). She advocates working with communities over time to help increase the community's capacity to accept returning children and better understand their experiences. The process involves developing collaborative programs with communities based on real involvement of community members. Community problem-solving, non-violent conflict resolution, community dialogue and mediation should be emphasized. Conflict resolution processes are key: "Education in the non-violent resolution of conflict permits one to express disagreement of opposition without resorting to violence. It opens the way for dialogue and negotiation…" (International Labour Office, 2003, p. 67). The mediation process occurs when a neutral third party facilitates negotiations between or among parties in conflict and assists the parties in reaching their own solutions that result in changed behaviour.

Gaining community acceptance of girls who return with babies, with ongoing dialogue and problem-solving, is described in this example from Sierra Leone:

> The communities were looking at these babies with disdain because the issue is there are certain rites [initiation, genital excision] that you should have gone through in the community for you to have a baby... if you have a baby without your parents giving you into marriage, then they look at it with a funny eye. And it is no fault of these girls that she has to have this child. And it is no fault to this baby that you have to bring forth this baby. So why deal with the baby that way? Therefore, there are always community meetings. They're always talking, they're always counselling—our own form of counselling: the informal way of meeting people, talking about them, bringing stories about what happened, what should not be, or what should happen. These were continued regularly. That is one of the programs we've used to be able to get this issue cleared (CCF staff interview, June 4, 2002).

In consideration of the study finding that "sensitization" is an imprecise process that should be transformed into result-based problem-solving, non-violent conflict resolution, dialogue with communities, and mediation when negotiations are required, the following recommendations are offered to improve the communication process on behalf of returnee girls:

POLICY RECOMMENDATIONS

Governments, the United Nations, multilateral agencies and INGOs should

> Use the mediation process, not "sensitization," in working with communities and focus upon behaviour change through results-based problem-solving, non-violent conflict resolution, and ongoing dialogue with communities.

> Support initiatives that enable community-based child protection workers to obtain a solid knowledge base in these behaviour-change processes, building upon local knowledge.

PROGRAM RECOMMENDATIONS

The governments of Sierra Leone and Uganda, donor governments, the United Nations and INGOs should

> Train child protection workers in non-violent conflict resolution skills and the mediation process, with a focus on results-based actions to maximize positive effects for girls. Include dialogue about gender and how the community understands it and how these constructions affect returnee girls.

Shame
FINDING:
Girls' shame should be dealt with by supporting girls' psychosocial healing, teaching girls and their communities about their rights, and promoting girls' self-efficacy.

Shame is an important cultural and gender variable that influences the healing process; its effects may be deep and prolonged. Scheff (1994) conceptualizes shame as a threat to the social bond and identifies it as the most social of all emotions that provides signals about one's standing in the moral universe. In a psychologically self-conscious state, one perceives oneself from the viewpoint of others.

Shame is a complex and powerful phenomenon that is often poorly understood or acknowledged at the cultural level. Its gendered dimensions are even less understood.

Agger (1992) studied refugee women in Denmark who had experienced political violence from state terrorism in countries they left behind. For the women she studied,

> A feeling of shame is also connected with acts which are dangerous and impure and which transgress boundaries. The woman's body as a whole comes to represent the dangerous area. And one who is careless, or not careful enough with her body, feels shame. We can see shame as the voice of society within the individual, "the silent speech that founds the social person" (Bidou, 1982, as cited in Agger, 1992, p. 24).

Agger (1992) characterized the power of shame as anything that endangers the accepted order. Situations that are labelled shameful and produce shameful feelings vary among cultures. In Western societies, the notion of shame often is deflected and called something else ("I feel hurt," "I am humiliated"), so that shame is conceived of as an individual experience. Within traditional societies, shame is something that happens to the community and family who are shamed by what happens—for example, the community has not adequately protected girls, and girls themselves also feel shame because what has happened to them, such as rape, violates community norms. Thus, shame may flow reciprocally between individual and community/family. Traditional rituals can be a way for both communities and individuals to begin to "undo the shame" by transforming stigmatized shame into re-integrative shame, the latter of which refers to the repair of social bonds (Errante, 1999).

In the three African countries we studied, girls in fighting forces have been forced to violate taboos more fully than boys within the context of gendered cultural dictates of sanctioned marriage, such as being shamed for underage and unmarried sex. For example, most girls were subject to gender-based sexual violence; many were forced into relationships with rebel captor-"husbands" and returned with children from the bush. This source of shame was acute in both Northern Uganda and Sierra Leone and was amplified when the baby was born of multiple rapes and without an identifiable father. An NGO child protection worker in Bo, Sierra Leone, characterized the shame that girls may face in speaking of one girl's experiences,

> ...she had a baby, this RUF, when she [was] raped. And when she was questioned by the parents, she couldn't tell them who the man was. She was not able to identify the man. All she knew was that the man was a rebel. And then later on, she found that she was pregnant, and she kept by herself. She didn't communicate with people. She didn't talk to anyone according to what the mother told us. She was really, really upset, and she was ashamed... And when the pregnancy showed, she was ashamed to be seen with the pregnancy (Sierra Leone, interview, June 6, 2002).

Another Sierra Leonean NGO worker who works with girls and women related that

> Women are more ashamed to accept that they are combatants, just as they are ashamed to say, "I was raped," because of the community's stigma. Sierra Leone is not ready for that (Sierra Leone, interview, June 7, 2002).

In a PHR report of war-related sexual violence, the most common reason women did not report attacks was because of "feelings of shame or social stigma (64 percent) and fear of being stigmatized or rejected (28 percent)" (PHR, 2002, p. 51). In Northern Uganda, a reintegration officer at a rehabilitation centre spoke of girls' shame,

> Shame, they feel guilty... They don't know what happened to them. When they come out, they are soldiers. Most girls don't want to be soldiers... and some of them are given to men when they were so young. They feel afraid. Even their "husbands" are always calling them names. They say, "You are a rebel, you are useless." They go back to their home [rather than through a rehabilitation centre], and how are they going to find another man? The girls need more help (Northern Uganda, interview, December 4, 2001).

Interestingly, a report by HRW concluded that because rape in Sierra Leone was so systematic and widespread and witnessed by many people, rape survivors—particularly those in urban areas—are not stigmatized and that most rape survivors are accepted joyfully back into their communities (January 2002). Although we agree that many girls were (or will be) welcomed back to their communities (if such still exist), the significant issue of stigma is being glossed over; indeed, this same HRW report found that many girls felt intense personal shame and anger, consistent with our findings.

Other sources of girls' shame are having identifiable tattoos, scars and carvings, and having participated in combat. Girls' shame also emanates from not being able to carry out traditional gender role behaviours such as menstrual hygiene and cleanliness and having engaged in taboo behaviours such as eating human flesh, seeing dead bodies and participating in brutal killings. Girls who entered into prostitution for economic survival, sometimes because their communities rejected them, also experience shame and isolation (Women's Commission, 2002). Such sources of shame speak to being an "accomplice to the forbidden" and threaten social identity (Agger, 1992, p. 8).

Within the context of their communities and families, girls can either silently live with their pain into their adult lives, or those who work with girls, their families and communities can assume the existence of shame and proactively address it. Strategies that can help alleviate shame include community rituals, the opportunity to share stories, acknowledging with sensitivity the normalcy of girls' responses, teaching girls about their rights, and providing assistance that empowers girls. Study recommendations are as follows:

PROGRAM RECOMMENDATIONS
Governments, the United Nations, multilateral agencies and INGOs should

> Build capacity within communities and child protection workers in communication skills that will enable them to better understand and respond to the psychological and social implications of girls' experiences, within the specific cultural context in which they are working.

> Support programs for girls that allow the expression of sadness and grief—emotions associated with shame. Girls can benefit from programs that encourage expression of their stories and concerns through drama, music and arts.

> Teach girls, their families and their communities about girls' rights.

> Provide opportunities for girls to enrol in school and/or skills training so that they develop a positive role within the community and personal self-efficacy, as a strategy to reduce feelings of shame. Such programs should provide incentives for pregnant girls and girl mothers to attend, e.g., feeding programs, day care and micro-economic schemes.

Reintegration Rituals
FINDING:
Community and religious rituals can help girls and their communities to heal.

Although distinct among the three countries and their regions studied, rituals were used to assist some girls in healing and reintegrating into their communities. Rituals can facilitate the process of healing, reconnect the child to the community of both living and dead and facilitate social reintegration. They may combine traditional and religious practices, or they may mix religious practices such as prayer, song and dance, and be used in preference to traditional practices. Depending on the context, those who conduct the rituals may be religious leaders, traditional healers, traditional leaders, or a combination. For example, in the northern part of Mozambique, especially in Nampula and Zambezia, ceremonies were performed by Muslim priests, who combined Muslim practices and praying with some local practices that are carried out by traditional healers. Similar findings appear in Angola, "Many people take a pluralistic approach to these healing rituals. They might submit themselves simultaneously to several healing strategies by going through 'traditional' rituals, church rituals as well as going to a hospital for treatment" (CCF Team in Angola, 1998, p. 85).

Among community-based rituals are those that welcome the child back, and cleansing rituals that drive out dead spirits, protect the community from contamination by evil influences and call upon the ancestors for assistance. The cleansing process is a fundamental condition of people's reintegration, especially in rural societies. The cleansing washes off the dangerous blood of war which can contaminate the community and cause insanity (Honwana, 1997, 2001, 2002; Wessells and Monteiro, 2003). A study in Angola found

> The performance of these rituals and the politics that precede them transcend the particular individuals concerned and involve the collective body. The family and friends are involved and the ancestral spirits are also implicated in mediating for a good outcome… the rituals are aimed at asking for forgiveness, appeasing the souls of the dead and preventing any future afflictions (retaliations) from the spirits of the dead, and in this way closing the links with that 'bad past.' (CCF Team in Angola, 1998, p. 85).

Girls often talked about rituals they went through when they returned home. In each of the study countries, distinct rituals existed. Our data indicate that rituals can support reintegration and healing for both the girl and the community. For example, a Northern Ugandan girl went through a combination of rituals when she returned home,

When she came back, she was made to step on an egg. Then they slaughtered a goat for her, and the community gathered to rejoice, and they took her to church. For four days they had a fasting in the church, showing her gratefulness to God for bringing her back home. After some time, they took her to town, and she was taken back to school (Northern Uganda, interview, November 26, 2001).

A PHR survey study in Sierra Leone (2002) in which 991 female heads of households participated found that 48 percent of respondents to a query about assistance to help one's "state of mind" said that traditional ceremonies were one such source. A World Health Organization (WHO) report (2003) on mental health in emergencies includes a recommendation to "encourage the re-establishment of normal cultural and religious events, including grieving rituals in collaboration with spiritual and religious practitioners" (WHO, 2003, p. 4). The report recommends that allopathic (medical) providers collaborate with traditional healers if feasible.

In Northern Uganda, ritual ceremonies have been reported to markedly impact children's ability to reconcile with their parents and to realize they are forgiven for their actions (Stavros, Stewart and Stavrou 2000). Errante (1999) observed that rituals in Mozambique worked to restore the person in the eyes of the community, to become as they were before offences occurred. These rituals contrast with Western modes of addressing trauma, which emphasize psychotherapeutic recounting and remembering experiences. Instead, rituals act to create a rupture with that past, as we were told in Mozambique—once you undergo the traditional ceremony, you are never allowed to speak of the trauma again. Likewise, stepping on an egg in Northern Uganda symbolizes taking on a new life.

In parts of Sierra Leone, rituals vary by region: some girls returning from a fighting force were given herb baths by traditional healers as a way to cleanse them. When economic means are insufficient to conduct rituals—for example, paying for a traditional healer or for a goat or chicken to slaughter or an egg to step on— participation in rituals may be impossible or substitute ceremonies may be created. In Northern Uganda, we were told that "prayer is cheaper."

Rituals, norms and encouragement: Rituals can be used to impose community normative behaviours—such as forbidding girls and their babies to be called "rebel wives" or "rebel babies," and laying the groundwork for not talking about what happened ("it is forgotten" or "don't think back, only look forward"). At Josina Machel Island in Mozambique, traditional leaders, with support from the local NGO, Rebuilding Hope, worked over time with children to help them deal with behavioural change and psychosocial issues, and to reintegrate into the community. When girls who were abducted by RENAMO forces returned to Josina Machel Island, they received advice along with a ritual:

> We would make a special braid for the girls and give them some advice about not having sex with lots of men and only to have sex when they are married. The braid would help them forget their bad experiences and memories and relieve their anger (Mozambique, interview, September 18, 2001).

In Sierra Leone, some Mammy Queens (female leaders of secret societies who may also be traditional midwives) combined ritual cleansing with "talk." Their strategy was to: "Talk to her, encourage her, embrace her, explain to her that she should be having hopes" (Sierra Leone, interview, June 11, 2002). In Northern Uganda, a 17-year-old girl told us that along with prayer, the leaders of her church visited her and told her she was a useful girl and should set a good example. She responded by thinking, "They believe in me, I thought I was useless. I was pregnant, but now I am free" (Uganda, interview, November 25, 2001). A 16-year-old Ugandan school girl told a similar story of church leaders praying, talking and giving advice. These strategies of social support in conjunction with rituals can aid children's social reintegration and facilitate positive psychosocial effects.

Gender-specific rituals: Importantly, some rituals for healing and community reintegration are gender specific. In Mozambique and Sierra Leone, rituals have helped heal sexually abused girls. Anthropologist Carolyn Nordstrom detailed a ritual for a woman in Mozambique who returned physically and emotionally traumatized (and presumably sexually abused) from a RENAMO base where she had been held for many months,

> Several high points included the ritual bath the woman received at dusk. Numerous women picked up the patient, and carefully gave her a complete bath—a cleansing of the soul as well as the body. The bathing was accompanied with songs and stories about healing, about dealing with trauma, about reclaiming a new life and being welcomed into the community. The patient was then dressed in her new clothing, and fed a nutritious meal… They carried her outside, where the community welcomed her as part of it… (Nordstrom, 1997, p. 145).

In Mozambique and Sierra Leone, we documented rituals for returning girls. Those in charge of these rituals are often old women. For example, in Mozambique, a rape ritual was described that was used to both cleanse and "vaccinate" the girl to reduce sexual desire. In Sierra Leone, Mammy Queens described a ritual for returning girls that used a special herb bath:

> Susan McKay (SM): Did you give herbs or do special ceremonies for the girls?
>
> Mammy Queen (through an interpreter): She say they went to the bush and get some medicine so they do what is known as cleansing.

SM: When a girl has bad dreams about what happened, would you be able to help her?

Mammy Queen (through an interpreter): She says she goes to the bush, get the hops, and she steams hops. Traditional sort of cleansing. They get the medicine, they heat it. Then you get cloth, cover all of your body. Then the steam that comes—it's a process of healing.

SM: Are the healing ceremonies different for boys and girls?

Mammy Queen (through an interpreter): She say with the men, it is different because they don't have the same place to cleanse them. They have their own separate area to go. The ladies have their own separate stream for the cleansing. So they are healed differently (Sierra Leone, interview, June 11, 2002).

At the same time, not all rituals are safe or appropriate. Some rituals violate the human rights of women and girls, reinforce patriarchy and oppressive gender roles (Mazurana and McKay, 1999), and support gender discrimination and sexism—such as the belief that women are the property of men. An example is when uninitiated girls reintegrate into communities in Sierra Leone. In such cases, initiation rituals with genital excision by female members of secret societies are necessary in order for a girl to be accepted back into society (see also Women's Commission, 2002). In Sierra Leone, the Amazonian Initiative Movement is an organization working to combat ritual practices of genital excision and to expose gender discrimination.

In consideration of these findings about traditional rituals in these three African societies, we offer the following recommendations:

PROGRAM RECOMMENDATIONS
International and local NGOs should

> Facilitate spiritual and religious rituals that do not violate or threaten the rights of women or girls or implicitly support or accept discrimination. The issue for the community is that spiritual contamination does not occur only for the child who returns but also for the community as a collective. Therefore, indigenous ritual practices can be positive for the community and support normalization and promote reconciliation.

> Recognize that communities and families in traditional societies may experience shame because they failed to protect their girls; therefore spiritual and religious rituals may be important for the community as well as for girls themselves. When they are contextually appropriate and safe, produce no further trauma, and do not contravene international human rights standards, rituals can be an important part of the healing process when children return to their communities.

> Support the initiatives of indigenous groups to address harmful ritual practices that violate children's and girls' human rights.

Empowering Girls
FINDING:
Girls' empowerment and strengths should be fostered in the post-war period.

The extremes of armed conflict affect children's identity development. Distressing experiences can result in a pessimistic view of life and the inability to conceive of a future for themselves (UN, 1996). Girls in fighting forces may experience what could be called "transition despair" when they leave a fighting force and/or a rebel captor-"husband." Girls may believe that they have no choices, no skills, and that there is no help for them, or "there is nothing to come out to." Girls ask, "Where would I go?" "What would I do?" The burden of an unwanted child and fear that they are not marriageable add to their feelings of powerlessness. Developing a sense of agency, self confidence and self esteem are therefore central for returning girls, particularly abducted girls and girl mothers.

Importantly, girls possess resiliency and agency that need to be recognized. Their strength comes through in stories such as having escaped captors (heard in all three countries), positioning themselves advantageously within a fighting force, and expressing personal defiance despite potentially negative consequences. Reinforcing the notion that girls' self-efficacy plays an important role when they are associated with fighting forces, Brett (2002) relayed how girl soldiers in Angola, Sri Lanka, the Philippines, and Colombia exhibited a strong sense of self or they would not have survived. Machel (2000) advocated that psychosocial support build upon this resilience. Harnessing girls' sense of power can affect the choices they make—if they are given effective assistance in the form of schooling, micro-credit schemes and skills training.

Programming: Jean-Claude Legrand of UNICEF emphasized that programs must promote the best interests of the child and should "enhance the self-esteem of the children, promote their capacity to protect their own integrity and to construct a position in life" (Legrand, 1999, p. 27). Programs must be developed using proper program principles, meaning that proper assessment of the situation of the girls and consulting with them are integral to program development. Further, programs should consider the child's age and stage of development and address the particular requirements of girls. Stavrou advocated training to enable staff at the GUSCO rehabilitation centre in Northern Uganda to support girls "on issues such as health education, including mental and reproductive health, and other support to build self-esteem and a positive perception about the future" (Stavrou et al., 2000, p. 22). To encourage girls' empowerment and build upon their strengths and resiliency, the following recommendations should be implemented:

POLICY RECOMMENDATIONS
Governments, the United Nations, multilateral agencies and INGOs should

> Prioritize support for girls by funding schooling, life skills training and economic schemes (for example, micro-credit programs, quick impact projects). Psychosocial programs should build upon girls' sense of agency, self esteem and confidence.

> Develop schools and training programs that are girl-friendly, have relevant curricula, and offer options such as accelerated ("catch up") programs to teach girls basic literacy and numerical skills, including accounting and other business skills. For example, FAWE's program in Sierra Leone promotes girls' education, includes pregnant girls and girl mothers who can attend school with their babies and/or children and proactively recruits disadvantaged girls.

> Engage girls in actively shaping, monitoring and evaluating these programs and making decisions about their futures.

> Make children's and women's rights, human rights, child protection, conflict resolution and peace education curricula integral to education and life skills training.

PROGRAM RECOMMENDATIONS
Governments, the United Nations, multilateral agencies and INGOs should

> Develop community-based programs that focus upon girls' strengths, self-efficacy and life skills, instead of their vulnerability and victimization. Variables such as girls' personalities, family situations and economic and psychosocial support should be considered during program planning.

> Involve male and female community elders and influential community members, who are protectors of the community and its best interests, when planning girls' programming; they are key individuals in helping girls resume normal lives within the community. Consult girls about who should be involved in program planning and implementation.

> Support indigenous community expressive arts that can provide culturally appropriate ways for girls to share their strengths and tell their stories, if the girls wish to do so. If they want to share their stories, ways to support and protect them should be developed.

> Provide girls with a range of learning options so they can become economically self-sufficient.

> Avoid segregating girls into "appropriate for gender" skills training. Programming earmarked for "boys" or "girls" can reinforce gender discrimination—for example, providing training for girls only in economically limited skills such as soap making and hair braiding instead of providing options for both traditional and non-traditional work, such as masonry, carpentry and welding.
> Assist girls who choose non-traditional work to find employment that does not discriminate against them because of gender.

Girl Mothers
FINDING:
Girl mothers and their babies and/or children are at high risk.

Within Northern Uganda and Sierra Leone, returnee girl mothers and their babies and/or children are highly vulnerable. The situation in Northern Uganda and Sierra Leone of babies and children who are born to girls in fighting forces is precarious: they are often stigmatized, lack basic health care, food, shelter and clothing, their mothers may have great difficulty providing for them, and attachment disorders between mothers and babies can affect the ability of these babies to thrive.

Faced with the evidence of rape (their children) and the violation of cultural taboos, combined with the responsibility of providing and caring for a baby or several children, girl mothers' choices are difficult. A key underlying factor that accounts for their vulnerability is that they very often find their own way back to their communities, where they and their children are hidden from outside help; consequently, they receive no assistance. Also, their numbers are underestimated, and international humanitarian groups have been insufficiently aware of their presence.

Adolescents in Northern Uganda identified being "child mothers as the largest problem affecting girls, and pointed out that it is especially common among abducted girls, who are also frequently treated as outcasts by the community if they manage to escape captivity" (RWC, 2001, p. 40). Stravou (2000) observed that in Northern Uganda, "even worse than sexual abuse is girls returning with babies of rebel commanders" (p. 20). These babies may be viewed as the "rebels of tomorrow" (UNICEF, unpublished manuscript). Not surprisingly, during the time that they are in a fighting force, girls are reported to abort pregnancies, abandon babies in hospitals or open fields, or commit infanticide (Djeddah, 1997; Mazurana and McKay, 2002; Mazurana et al., 2002). Even when girl mothers are welcomed back by families and communities, their babies are often poorly accepted. If the father is unknown, the stigma is greater. In Sierra Leone, some girls go back and forth between their communities and their captor-"husbands."

Girls with babies and orphaned girls are at great risk of entering the sex trade or becoming part of organized prostitution. Girls who enter the sex trade represent a failure of proper programming for them. Their dire economic situation, however, often provides few options for survival except for sex work. Also, family members may push girls into the sex trade to assure their economic survival (Women's Commission, 2003; Sierra Leonean study data; UN High Commission on Refugees [UNHCR] and Save the Children/United Kingdom [SC/UK], 2002). Cultural factors affect whether babies are accepted, for example, matrilineal vs. patrilineal societies, although notions of whether the baby belongs to the father or mother's family are complicated. At Josina Machel Island in Mozambique, babies born of forced sex were accepted as belonging to the mother (although this may vary elsewhere in Mozambique), whereas in Northern Uganda and Sierra Leone, babies born of rebel fathers are often poorly accepted. In Northern Uganda, girls

> ...do not like the unwanted babies; many of these mothers are young and want to go to school but they can't because of the kids. Flashback of their attacks torment many of these young mothers (Barton, Mutiti and Assessment Team, 1998, p. 33).

At risk is the healthy development of children born of forced maternity, although almost no concerted attention has been paid to this vulnerable group. A nurse who works in a rehabilitation centre health clinic in Northern Uganda spoke of hardships faced by children born of rebel fathers, "It's difficult because they grow up... I do not know what kind of generation we're going to have with these children because [of] years of living in the bush, no culture, nothing." She expressed concern about the maternal behaviours of returnee girls,

> In our culture [Acholi], you are not supposed to deny your child... Sometimes when the child is crying and irritated, the woman [mother] will blow up...'I hate you, I wish you could die.' So in some ways, there's no attachment. And they don't want to identify with these children... They don't want a close link with the babies. We try to tell them it's not the baby's fault. But in most cases, they leave them with their mothers (Josephine Amogm interview, December 4, 2001).

As emphasized by Carpenter (2000), forced pregnancy has been treated as a women's issue but should also be considered a children's rights' issue.

> Children have a right not to be stigmatized or neglected as a result of their origins; and deliberately conceiving a child whose mother's victimization will bring about its own suffering, and loss of life chances should be treated as a crime. International law should be equipped to articulate, reach and punish such harms; and the NGO sector should be empowered to address the needs of these children as well as the needs of rape victims and their communities (Carpenter, 2000, p. 9).

Carpenter emphasized the importance of changing community norms to stop rejection and stigmatization of children born of rape by targeting their mothers to encourage them to accept and care for their children.

A UNHCR and SC-UK assessment mission in Guinea, Liberia, and Sierra Leone, although focused on refugee camps, similarly found that girl mothers as a group had few or no programs targeted to help them (UNHCR and SC-UK, 2002). Chronic inattention and under-funding of programs for pregnant girls and girls with babies and or children are indicative of sexism. In consideration of these findings, the following actions should be taken:

POLICY RECOMMENDATIONS
Governments, the United Nations, multilateral agencies and INGOs should

> Fund longitudinal research to learn how babies and children of girls who return from fighting forces fare in their physical, psychological and relational development and work out the best ways to help them thrive.

> Develop preventive policies and programs to plan ahead to receive and assist returning girls (psychosocial, health and economic initiatives).

> Fund programming initiatives that focus upon girl sex workers: family tracing, reconciliation and reintegration counselling, reunification, health care, health education including the prevention of STDs, skills training, and, especially, income-generating activities and revolving funds. Economic skills are critical to get girls out of sex work. Establish infrastructures such as mobile medical clinics and drop-in centres to reach girl sex workers/prostitutes. Night clinics can increase accessibility to services, which is important because these girls may work at other jobs during the day or be taking care of their children.

PROGRAM RECOMMENDATIONS
The governments of Northern Uganda and Sierra Leone and INGOs should

> Focus on health and psychosocial programming for girls and their babies and/or children as a high priority, with long-term follow up of this highly vulnerable population.

> Involve the immediate families of these girls in discussions about health. The family can offer support and assist with long-term planning for the girl's future.

> Support community-based organizations to start up mutual support groups for girls with babies based on income generation, health, child welfare and psychosocial assistance.

> Link girls to women's groups for psychosocial support and assistance in learning mothering skills.

Rebel Captor-"Husbands"
FINDING:
Returning girls face difficulties because of rebel captor-"husbands."

A girl with a baby and a rebel captor-"husband" who might potentially marry her according to community customs of marriage and dispute settlement can be socially positioned more advantageously than a girl reintegrating with a baby and no "husband." If her captor-"husband" is accepted by her family and community, she avoids the great cultural fear that she is not wanted by a man or that she might not have a husband. Girls are sometimes told that staying with rebel captor-"husbands" is in their best interests (and sometimes it may be) or they may view this as their best, and perhaps only, option. According to an INGO child protection worker with extensive experience in helping girls return to their communities,

> …we have to recognize that maybe these girls… were taken quite young, and they don't see any other option, but they do consider the men to be their husbands, even if they don't necessarily want to be with that man. They still consider him to be their legitimate husband in some way. And it's older people and outside people who are saying that's not a legitimate marriage: just because you've been with him and you've been sleeping with him and you have a child, it's not a marriage [they say]. He is supposed to go to your parent's house and ask for you and do these things, which is what many NGOs have been encouraging and [also] what we've [INGO] been encouraging… But the concept that they are wives and that these are their men is quite strong for them… they don't perceive themselves… [as] at this point still held against their will… They're choosing to stay with men because they have no idea who possibly else would want to take care of them, and they've been told that nobody else would want them (Catherine Wiesner interview, June 5, 2002).

Reflecting a patriarchal view of women's situation in Sierra Leone, a female child protection worker with the NCDDR in Sierra Leone explained the issue,

> I saw things differently than they saw. It's like the child protection agencies… the approach they used was wrong in the first place… in trying to get these girls out. The girls were abducted, yes. This is a terrible crime, yes. They were raped, yes. They have been impregnated, yes. But over the years this may have… provided a certain amount of security for them. This man has protected them. This man has been provided for them. So a bond has starting existing between the woman and the man. They've had children now. And it's like, what can a woman go back to, or what can a child go back to? She now has a child with this man. Maybe she has a town [that] has burnt down. Her parents have been killed… Even if they go back, what will they go back to? Can my mother now take care of me and my two children? We're all women, we all want some amount of security, and we all want a man who can take care of us (Sierra Leone, interview, June 5, 2002).

Such thinking can affect the establishment of meaningful gender-sensitive programming that is intended to empower girls instead of reinforcing gender discrimination. Another Sierra Leonean informant, who worked for an INGO that focuses upon women and children, differed in her thinking,

> If you've been abducted and you had a bush husband, you come back, people know that you've been abducted... it's a stigma. So for them, because of the pressure and the fear of not getting a husband, they may just decide to stay with that man... But given the preference, if she had another husband, had somebody else who had come forward, who did not abduct her... another choice... [a man] who did not beat her, who did not put her through all that she went through. My guess is she would pick that man, they [girls] fear they will never get a husband. In this country that is a big, big fear for women. Even [for] educated women (Binta Mansaray interview, June 7, 2002).

Helping girls leave: Some girls need help getting away from their captor-"husbands." Because of economic and social factors (such as whether she will be accepted if she returns to her community with a baby/children), girls can face the difficult choice of staying with their bush captor-"husbands" or involving themselves in unorganized sex work or engaging in prostitution (Women's Commission, 2002). A study of adolescents in Sierra Leone found that,

> Most [girls] remain attached to 'bush husbands' even if they have gone through ICCs [Interim Care Centre]... if their bush husbands came around, the girls would increasingly do things with them outside the ICCs... At the same time, some adolescent mothers interviewed who had gotten away from their 'bush husbands' and found support from their families said they did not want to be with these men anymore. Interestingly, however, they said they would take money from them to help support their children (Women's Commission, 2002, p. 61).

Girls with rebel captor-"husbands" must be treated with sensitivity to their individual contexts and given support and opportunities to make choices that are best for them, instead of being either forced to leave bush husbands or given so little economic and psychosocial support that they have no choice but to stay with them. In consideration of these findings, we recommend the following actions:

PROGRAM RECOMMENDATIONS
Grassroots groups, national NGOs and INGOs should

> Emphasize girls' rights, resources, and assistance needs and help them to understand and explore their options. Because numerous factors affect girls' decisions and actions in their relationships with rebel captor-"husbands," they must be given time and support to make their own decisions.

> Involve parents, or their stand-ins, as an important aspect of the girl's long-term security. A girl's parents may need to be involved in her decisions, especially if she truly wishes to marry her captor-"husband." Parents, or their stand-ins, will continue to play an important role in the girl's long-term security.
> Prioritize assistance for girl mothers who have been abandoned by rebel captor-"husbands" or who choose not to return to them.
> Develop innovative programming to help girls become self sufficient—for example, interim group homes, and homes for pregnant girls and girl mothers to receive physical and psychosocial assistance and to learn economic skills, and school programs that enrol pregnant girls and girls with babies/children. Community-based solutions should be given priority.
> Organize girls' solidarity groups for income-generating activities and build in emotional and social support. When these young mothers are brought together, they can talk about their problems, hopes and modes of adapting.

Sexual Violence
FINDING:
Nearly all abducted girls are raped, and girls associated with fighting forces almost universally report sexual violence.

Sexual violence against women during armed conflicts has been widely documented throughout the world (see, for example, Barton, Mutiti, et al., 1998; Brownmiller, 1975; Isis-WICCE, 2001, 2002; Lindsey, 2001; Lorentzen and Turpin, 1998; McKay, 1998; PHR, 2002; Sajor, 1998; Shan Human Rights Foundation and Shan Action Network, 2002; UN, 1995; 1996; 2002). Although boys, too, are subject to sexual violence, the frequency is low in comparison to girls. Admitting that sexual violence towards boys has occurred is even more taboo than is rape of girls, especially because it may involve homosexual behaviour (Josephine Amogm interview, December 4, 2001). In Sierra Leone, boys were reported to have been sexually abused by girls when a group of abducted girls outnumbered the boys (CCF Staff interview, June 4, 2002). McConnan and Uppard (2001) observed that little recognition has been given to date to the fact that boys are also affected by sexual violence, with poor understanding of the impacts.

Our study findings are consistent with previous reports about the widespread prevalence of sexual violence towards girls and women. In the three African countries, rape was reported as happening to virtually all abducted girls, although some small girls were spared, as were some who were taken only briefly. Gang rape and sexual torture were prevalent experiences of abducted girls who were used for sex by many men, often during a single day. "Wives" of rebel captor-"husbands" sometimes received protection from broader sexual violence because of these liaisons.

The widespread rape of girls in Northern Uganda and Sierra Leone has been documented by HRW (January 2003; March 2003) and other human rights groups (AI, 1997; PHR, 2002). In both countries, we heard similar stories about sexual violence, sometimes related by girls who volunteered this information. Our primary informants regarding sexual violations were NGO and UN workers, professionals such as nurses and teachers, and women within communities (for example, women activists in Mozambique and Mammy Queens in Sierra Leone) because we chose, as part of the CIDA/Rights & Democracy interview protocol, not to directly ask girls about sexual violence.

Girls rarely report sexual violence because of its stigma and their sense of shame (Glenis Taylor interview, May 31, 2001; Machel, 2000). Stavrou and colleagues (2000) reported that during interviews they conducted in Northern Uganda with young female adolescent ex-abductees, a state of denial was evident. Also, sexual abuse is seldom discussed within communities. In Northern Uganda, explicit discussion of sexual violence is unusual, even though its occurrence is widely known and escalating levels of sexual violence are currently being reported in Northern Uganda (see for example, HRW, July 2003). In public discourse and within communities, an emphasis should be placed upon the culpability of the perpetrator rather than the girls in order to shift the debate about sexual violence to focus upon those who are responsible.

In post-war Sierra Leone, girls are often at high risk of being raped, even within their own communities (see for example, interview with Claire Fatu Hanciles as cited in HRW, 2002). In all three countries, a climate of impunity about rape exists. As emphasized by Machel (2000), impunity for war crimes committed against children, including rape, must end.

Few support services for rape survivors and rape prevention programs exist. As noted by PHR (2002), some local and international NGOs have developed services for rape survivors, but they can assist only a fraction of girls affected; most programs are located in Freetown, such as programs established by UNICEF for raped girls who have become mothers (PHR, 2002; Glenis Taylor interview, May 31, 2001). Glenis Taylor, Child Protection Officer at UNICEF in Sierra Leone, discussed how difficult it has been for girls and communities to talk about sexual violence. Taylor has worked with communities within the Freetown area to help them accept these girls,

> We went out into all the communities, this was primarily in the Western area [of Sierra Leone] saying 'if you have been raped, please come out and say I have been raped. People and neighbours, committee members, don't point fingers at the girls. It's not their fault that they were raped. It could have happened to anyone'... and encouraging them to come forward, saying... 'it wasn't you, but it could so easily have been you. So even if you know of someone who has been raped, don't laugh at them but try to encourage them to come forward'... so things improved a bit after that (Glenis Taylor interview, May 31, 2001).

An example of NGO programming is a CCF program called "Sealing Our Past, Securing Our Future" for sexually abused girls. In communities where CCF works, sexual violence committees have been established, comprised of people within the community who are responsible for negotiating, advocating and dealing with past and present sexual violence issues. Another example is the long-term sexual and gender-based violence programs established in camps for internally displaced persons in eastern and southern Sierra Leone (HRW, January 2002). UNICEF, Sierra Leone, in collaboration with its child protection partners, has supported the development of regional committees to deal specifically with sexual and gender-based violence, a major change since 1999, because previously, rape and sexual violence were not talked about (Donald Robertshaw interview, May 31, 2002). Also, IRC has begun sexual violence programs and clinics in Freetown and in refugee camps where the organization works (Courtney Mireille O'Connor, personal communication, August 8, 2003).

"Rape talk" in the media: The power of the media, when used constructively, can be an important and effective means of addressing gender discrimination, sexism and violence against girls and women. Lifting taboos against talking about rape is a major social change from prevalent practices and has the potential to expose and help prevent the prevalence of gender-based violence during and after war. Women are increasingly using the media at the local, national and international level towards this goal (McKay and Mazurana, 2001).

In Sierra Leone, past sexual abuse during the war and current sexual abuse are discussed on national and, sometimes, on community radio, especially within urban areas. Cause Canada of Sierra Leone works with radio stations to produce regular programming that has featured girls telling their own stories (Jeffrey Kyle and Maureen Urquhart interview, May 29, 2002). MAMA, a radio station for women sponsored by the Uganda Media Women's Association, raises issues about violence against women, including violence against women in Northern Uganda, and features women's stories about their life circumstances (Uganda Media Women's Association interview, November 21, 2001).

Much more programmatic attention must be addressed towards working on the issue of gender-based sexual violence. The following actions should be taken in an effort to more effectively assist sexually abused girls and better protect their human rights, including through prevention:

POLICY RECOMMENDATIONS
Governments, the United Nations, multilateral agencies and INGOs should

> Step up training of government armed forces, security forces and peacekeeping forces on children's rights, protection of children and women's rights. Training should be instituted both during and after armed conflict.

> Train personnel within DDR programs, interim care centre staff, and other front-line groups that will interact with returning girls in the areas of children's rights, protection of children, and women's rights. Training should be based on national policies and international standards about how sexual violence should be addressed.

> Prosecute violators for gender-based crimes and sexual violence against girls in situations of armed conflict. Take steps to make sure that national and international legal systems provide accessible and gender-sensitive redress.

PROGRAM RECOMMENDATIONS
Governments, the United Nations, grassroots groups and INGOs should

> Train front-line health and psychosocial workers in identification and referral, within the context of broader assistance programs, of girls who have had their rights violated through sexual and gender-based violence.

> Develop programs in or near conflict areas to work with girls who have experienced sexual violence.

> Direct program initiatives towards babies born as a result of sexual violence as a priority. Those with unidentified fathers may be at high risk because of maternal rejection, which can cause poor emotional attachment. Communities may also reject these children. Pregnancies resulting from sexual violence usually occur in very high-stress environments with inadequate nutrition and health care, with high likelihood of maternal-infant transfer of STDs, thus placing the mothers and babies at even greater risk.

> Educate girls about their rights and encourage them to participate in actions that increase their own sexual protection.

> Encourage and fund public discourse to increase awareness of sexual violence, women's/girls' rights to personal security, and reduce persistent taboos against "not talking." Radio and television stations and print media can air girls' stories as told by the girls themselves and use creative programming such as soap operas to convey messages about sexual abuse, sexually transmitted diseases stigma, and other child protection issues faced by girls.

> Include public awareness programs about boys' sexual abuse, suffering, and needs.

Sexually Transmitted Diseases
FINDING:
Girls associated with fighting forces are at high risk for sexually transmitted diseases (STDs) and reproductive services are seldom available to them.

Not surprisingly, given the extent of sexual violence, the majority of girls returning from fighting forces have STDs, including syphilis, gonorrhoea, chlamydia, and HIV/AIDS. Extensive genital damage, including that resulting from genital excision rituals as practiced in Sierra Leone, increases girls' vulnerability to STDs and HIV/AIDS (Mazurana, McKay, Carlson and Kasper, 2002; PHR, 2002; RWC, 2002). Infections can lead to pelvic inflammatory disease, chronic pain and infertility.

Few girls are diagnosed and treated unless they go through a rehabilitation or interim care centre where these services are provided, or if an NGO has established community-based primary medical care. Even when services are available, they are not designed for girls. Further, an almost total absence of sexual and reproductive health services exists in the three countries where we conducted fieldwork. According to a report from Save the Children, "In Sierra Leone, 62 percent of peripheral health units do not function... [the] National STI Treatment Service workers in Connaught Hospital in Freetown lacked the recommended treatment for gonorrhoea and had to issue prescriptions for the treatment of choice, Ciprofloxacin, that many could not afford" (2002, pp. 15-16).

In Mozambique, traditional beliefs and practices have been found to run counter to HIV/AIDS campaigns. For example, in Zambezia province, youth believe that a sexually transmitted disease can be cured by having sex: the "bad spirit" moves out to another body and you are healed (Sayagues, 2000). Similarly, most adolescents surveyed in Port Loko, Sierra Leone, did not believe in the existence of many diseases, especially HIV/AIDS (Women's Commission, 2002). Also, condom use in Sierra Leone is low (American Refugee Committee Survey, 2001, as cited in Women's Commission, 2002). Testing for STDs is seldom available or may not be offered, and education in prevention is rare. An adolescent-directed study in Sierra Leone (Women's Commission, 2002) found that, among other reasons, the spread of STDs has occurred because of social disintegration, multiple population displacements, intravenous drug use, and the presence of foreign troops and peacekeepers, whose own infection rates are high and who therefore contribute to increased infection rates among girls to whom they pay money for sex. Sub-Saharan Africa, especially southern Africa, is by far the worst-affected region in the world (Rehn and Sirleaf, 2002; UN Programme on HIV/AIDS [UNAIDS], 1998, 2002).

A study by ISIS-WICCE (1998) of major causes of illness in sexually assaulted women in Luwero District, Northern Uganda, during the war that occurred there between 1980 and 1986, reported that 33 percent of 88 female respondents suffered from sexually transmitted diseases (STDs). Two ISIS-WICCE reports of studies conducted in Gulu District, Northern Uganda between 1986 and 1999 observed that STDs in girls were quite common (ISIS-WICCE, 2001a, 2001b). Josephine Amogn, a nurse at the World Vision rehabilitation centre in Northern Uganda reported that, based upon her clinical experience at the centre in Gulu, "all of them [girls] come with a kind of STD" (interview, December 4, 2001). A research officer at GUSCO in Gulu City reported that almost 80 percent of girls coming back from long periods in captivity return with STDs, including HIV/AIDS (Northern Uganda, interview, December 3, 2001). In Sierra Leone, of 94 women surveyed who reported war-related sexual violence, 34 percent self-reported STDs (PHR, 2002). According to a UN report (2002, February), 70 to 90 percent of rape survivors in Sierra Leone had contracted STDs, with abducted girls at particular high risk because of the many episodes of sexual violence. In Mozambique, STDs were less a feature of the war than a contemporary phenomenon, as STDs, particularly HIV/AIDS, have escalated because of cross-border migration—particularly of male Mozambican workers returning from work in the mines in South Africa.

Self-reports, as were used in the ISIS-WICCE and PHR studies, give only a glimpse of the actual incidence of STDs, because many girls and women do not know from their symptoms that they have an STD or may be unwilling to share this information. Because testing for STDs is not usually available in Northern Uganda or Sierra Leone, clinical examinations supply only partial diagnostic evidence, and girls' access to health care is extremely limited, the actual incidence of STDs in Northern Uganda and Sierra Leone is unknown. A "best guess" is that most returning girls are infected with one or more STDs.

HIV/AIDS: Machel (2000) highlighted the extreme threat to children of HIV/AIDS and the intensification of this threat when wars occur. Until anti-retroviral drugs become available, treatment is palliative at best. Estimated numbers of children between birth and 14 years of age living with HIV/AIDS at the end of 2001 for the three study countries are as follows: Mozambique, 80,000 (reflecting the current situation rather than being war related); Sierra Leone, 16,000; and Uganda, 110,000 (UNICEF, 2002). At the end of 2001 in Mozambique, 420,000 children between birth and 14 years were estimated to be orphans because of HIV/AIDS. In Sierra Leone, the estimated number is 42,000 and in Uganda, 880,000 (UNICEF, 2002). A PHR report noted that abductees are particularly vulnerable, "Of 17 girls voluntarily taken by their parents to the National AIDS Control Program [in Sierra Leone] for testing in 1999/2000, 10 were positive" (PHR, 2000).

Gender inequality and economic deprivation are major factors driving the HIV/AIDS epidemic (UNAIDS, 2002). Girls are at particular risk in conflict situations because of repeated rape and genital trauma (PHR, 2000), compounded by an acute lack of knowledge and denial of HIV/AIDS (SC, 2002). Babies of abducted returnee girls are also at risk because of mother-to-child transmission of HIV/AIDS during pregnancy and childbirth and from breast milk. About one-third of HIV mother-to-child transmissions are attributable to breast feeding (UNAIDS, 2002). In Northern Uganda and Sierra Leone, the few girls who are tested and found to be HIV positive do not have access to treatment, other than supportive counselling. Although the prevalence of HIV/AIDS is unknown among former abductees, at WV, of 83 children who chose to be tested, 13 (seven girls and six boys) were HIV positive, or 15.66 percent. Three of the seven girls were mothers. At GUSCO, two of 11 children who chose to be tested were HIV positive, or 7 percent (HRW, July 2003).

Prevention and treatment must be a focus of international, regional, and national policy and programmatic attention. Returnee girls and their children are at great risk of infection from STDs, especially HIV/AIDS. The Mano River Women's Peace Network in West Africa has emphasized the importance of creating and enhancing public awareness of STDs, especially HIV/AIDS, and the importance of HIV counselling and testing and programs for prevention and treatment (Femmes Africa Solidarité, 2000). Actions to meet this urgent threat include the following:

POLICY RECOMMENDATIONS
Governments, the United Nations, multilateral agencies and INGOs should

> Prioritize STD health education and prevention programs for funding and implementation. Develop much more rigorous HIV/AIDS programming in war-affected areas, including programs to heighten community awareness and to provide home-based care.

> Offer all returning girls and their babies testing and treatment for STDs, following country consent procedures and policies. Provide support services for when girls learn testing results and during long-term follow-up.

> Recognize that HIV/AIDS is a major threat to girl mothers and their babies/children. Many mothers will die, leaving their children orphaned.

> Work within the broader framework of African HIV/AIDS prevention and treatment programs so that these girls and their babies/children have long-term health and psychosocial care, with safety nets developed for orphaned children and children with affected parents who must act as the heads of their households.

> Prioritize support services for all girls at satellite outreach clinics and within communities where girls can be followed over time. Girls must have ongoing relationships with care providers who can support them in facing up to positive test results and helping them plan their lives and those of their children.
> Negotiate programs for rapid treatment of STDs for girls and babies within the framework of "days of tranquility" campaigns.

PROGRAM RECOMMENDATIONS
Governments, the United Nations, multilateral agencies and INGOs should

> Provide "girl friendly" reproductive health care services with well-trained female workers and access for all returning girls at demobilization sites, satellite outreach clinics and within communities. Mobile units in urban and rural areas and satellite health clinics are important outreach strategies.
> Involve girls in deciding best locations, opening hours and preferred modes of health care delivery.
> Train and utilize community women elders, psychosocial workers and health workers to help with identification, referral for treatment and follow-up of girls with sexual or reproductive health problems and to promote behaviour change.
> Ensure confidentiality of testing results and treatment.
> Target war-affected countries in Africa for concentrated implementation assistance because they have the greatest need. HIV/AIDS programs in Africa have developed a wide range of policies in cooperation with the World Health Organization, but they have the weakest implementation of these policies. Implementation may be focused in non-war affected parts of the country, as in Uganda, but nonexistent in the war-affected areas as, for example, in Northern Uganda.
> Provide condoms and other barrier devices to reduce the spread of STDs during armed conflict and after the fighting stops, to be distributed without consideration of political or ideological affinity. However, condom distribution is sensitive and must be handled according to governmental regulations.
> Plan programs to educate girls and promote behaviour change with respect to condom use, because girls may be reluctant to ask sexual partners to use them.
> Educate and empower boys and men to choose sexual responsibility over macho/patriarchal denial and aggression.

Physical and Psychological Health
FINDING:
Girls suffer gender-specific physical and psychological health problems.

Infant and child mortality rates in a country are critical indicators of the well-being of its children. Using UNICEF data as a gauge, children's health status in the three countries where we conducted fieldwork are among the worst in the world (UNICEF, 2003). Sierra Leone ranks as the worst in the world for child mortality under the age of five, with 316 deaths per 1000; its infant mortality rate (deaths in the first year of life) for 2001 was 182 deaths per 1000 live births (UNICEF, 2003). A study by IRC, issued in February 2001, found that, in the Kenema District of the Eastern province of Sierra Leone, the infant mortality rate was 303 deaths per 1000 live births (Ministry of Health and Sanitation, Sierra Leone, and IRC Health Unit, 2001). One finding from the study was that a relatively low percentage of infants were under one year—only 3 percent of the population, whereas 5 or even 6 percent is more usual. This is potentially explainable because of the high infant mortality rate. Another explanation comes from a report from PHR that cited an interview with a physician in the town of Kenema. Returning abductee mothers, he said, were bringing babies so sick and malnourished that 20 to 50 percent were dying in the hospital (PHR, 2000). Undoubtedly, many of these returnee mothers were girls and countless more infants died in the bush.

Mozambique is ranked twelfth worst in the world for child mortality under the age of five, which was estimated to be 197 children per 1000 in 2001; for the same year, its infant mortality rate was 125 per 1000 (UNICEF, 2003). Uganda's estimated 2001 child mortality rate was 124 per 1000 (thirty-sixth worst in the world), with an infant mortality rate of 79 per 1000 (UNICEF, 2003). Poverty and the effects of armed conflicts, including the lack of public health infrastructure to provide basic human needs such as food, water, health care and housing, are key reasons for these dismal figures. In Northern Uganda, medical supplies, high hospital fees, poor performance and corruption of some health workers and unevenly distributed hospitals all contribute to limited health care access (Women's Commission, 2001). A primary health care unit that we visited in Gulu District consisted of a small room with two nurses seeing patients who waited in a long line outside for hours, some with obviously serious health problems. At one end of the room was a curtain, behind which a woman was in labour. Occasionally, a nurse pulled back the curtain slightly to check her progress. At a hospital in the Apac District of Northern Uganda where we interviewed the medical director, part of the facility had been destroyed by LRA forces and the pharmacy contained almost no medicines. The "laboratory" was a table with one microscope.

Health problems: Returnee children, both boys and girls, commonly experience health problems such as malaria, tuberculosis, cholera, diarrhoea, parasitic infections and malnutrition, and war-related injuries that range from chronic health problems to severe disabilities, loss of sight, hearing, amputation of limbs, and scars or burns from torture or injuries inflicted during battle. Notably, children with disabilities fare poorly as returnees. Adolescents in Northern Uganda reported that those with disabilities experience particular difficulties in accessing health care (Women's Commission, 2001). In Sierra Leone, children with disabilities "tended to be left behind by the factions on manoeuvres and left to make their own way back to their communities" (UNICEF, unpublished report, p. 43).

The leading cause of death of children in many war zones is lack of sanitation and health care (Schaller, 1995). In the three study countries, as regularly occurs in war zones, hospitals and clinics were destroyed, medicines looted, nursing and medical personnel targeted and/or abducted to provide services to rebel forces, and supplies taken. Midwives in villages have also reportedly been taken by fighting forces. An elderly Mammy Queen midwife in Sierra Leone was abducted by the RUF to provide health care. She explained:

> When they [RUF] go to the communities, they don't just capture those communities—they go around looking for some of these facilities, like medicine in the hospital. So there are people who go there and loot, take them to the bush. They have captured doctors, TBAs (traditional birth attendants), MCHA (maternal child health aides) (Mammy Queen interview, June 11, 2002).

Health problems of returnee girls: The most common problems reported by girls were headaches (from beatings and psychological causes), anxiety and nervousness, "stomach ache" (lower abdomen—possibly from STDs and/or pelvic inflammatory disease), effects of drug use, scabies and skin diseases, chest pain, pain from beatings, symptoms of genital injury or infection, including swelling, fistulas, vaginal discharge, genital itch, pain from the vagina being cut, and trauma to the genital and anal regions and bladder from sexual abuse.

Girls testified about the psychological effects of fear, worry and anxiety related to concerns such as not having a husband, not knowing where to go, nobody wanting them, not having options, and seeing a bleak future with little hope. Girls spoke of broken hearts—that you can die of a broken heart: "Medically you can be ill; you be healed. But broken hearts… they are very difficult to mend. How can you mend your broken hearts? What kind of assistance you need in that?" (Sierra Leone, interview, June 11, 2002). Girls clearly need psychosocial assistance in tandem with practical help to meet basic needs such as food, shelter and medicine.

Some girls were reported to be aggressive, quarrelsome and compulsive when they returned. In contrast, other girls withdrew and did not speak about their experiences. A deaf girl, living in a fostering situation in Sierra Leone discussed her psychological difficulties through an interpreter:

> She says sometimes she's traumatized, and she'd like to talk to someone. When she's traumatized, most times she cries. She needs to talk sometimes when she's lonely. And she thinks of all she has gone through. And she sometimes sits all alone, without talking to anyone. Not even wanting to... she doesn't even want to see anyone (Sierra Leone, interview, June 6, 2002).

Girls' health, both physical and psychological, has received insufficient attention. Although primary health care delivery within Sierra Leone is dismal at best, girls' health is at particular risk because of gender discrimination, lack of access (especially for girls who live in rural areas), their age, and injuries to their reproductive organs. To begin to improve their access, treatment and health status, the following actions are required:

POLICY RECOMMENDATIONS
Governments, the United Nations, multilateral agencies and INGOs should

> Gather systematic data about girls' health problems and long-term physical and psychological health issues to better identify and care for girls' health problems upon their return.

> Fund the development of health care infrastructures in Northern Uganda and Sierra Leone, with services specifically for girls.

PROGRAM RECOMMENDATIONS
Governments, the United Nations, multilateral agencies and INGOs should

> Offer free medical screening and care and accompanying health care support services to all returning children and develop links with referral services.

> Offer free medical screening and health care to all returning girls, with an emphasis on reproductive health care and psychosocial assistance.

> Provide health education to girls, including child care, as part of the rehabilitation process.

> Develop cooperative arrangements with local and national health services to ensure sustainable, long-term health care systems.

Pregnancy and Childbirth Risks
FINDING:
Girls and their babies often die or are physically disabled because of pregnancy-related problems

Just as infant mortality is an indicator of children's well-being, maternal mortality is an indicator of women's well-being. Pregnancy and childbirth outcomes in each of the three countries are among the worst in the world, as indicated by 1985–2001 estimated maternal mortality rates per 100,000 births: Sierra Leone, 1800; Uganda, 510; Mozambique,1100 (UNICEF, 2002). Social and political violence have been shown to significantly raise the risk of pregnancy complications (Zapata, Rebolledo, Atalah, Newman and King, 1992). Sierra Leone ranks among the bottom ten countries in terms of maternal well-being; one consequence is that a mother's risk of dying during pregnancy and childbirth is more than 600 times greater than mothers who live in countries ranked within the top ten (SC, 2003). Yet, in talking to girls themselves, denial of abortions and maternal and infant deaths was common. High, even catastrophic, levels of complications and deaths of girls and/or their infants were reported during interviews with indigenous NGO and grassroots workers.

For girls of childbearing age and women, war heightens the risk of maternal and infant death. This is because of the difficult conditions they face and also because mothers and infants are often purposely targeted for torture and death by fighting forces, whether or not they are in these forces. Pregnant girls and women and mothers (sometimes with babies wrapped on their backs and drugged with cocaine to keep them quiet) participated in fighting. At the Conforti Home for mothers in Freetown, staff members reported:

> If commanders did not want children because it was an extra mouth to feed and would slow down the group, they would sometimes not take care of the women or even abort the babies. We have a lot of girls who died as a result of this kind of thing. Some of them did not have medical care and died in the process of delivering. Most of their friends died in the bush when they were going to deliver (Conforti Home Staff interview, June 14, 2002).

Yet, maternity can also protect women from violence. For example, in Southern Sudan, a special LRA camp (Nsitu) previously existed for mothers with babies and children. Camps like it, sometimes called "breeder camps," provided a measure of security and basic needs for mothers and children, and as children grew older, they were recruited into the LRA. In Sierra Leone, some girls with children benefited from comparative protection by rebel captor-"husbands." Other pregnant girls were released from the RUF and taken to safer areas.

Especially in Northern Uganda and Sierra Leone, atrocities against pregnant girls/women and new mothers and their infants were reported. In Sierra Leone and Northern Uganda, babies or children were reportedly left behind at health clinics or with captor-"husbands" or their other wives in the bush when the girl escaped. Unknown numbers of babies and children died in the bush or were killed by rebels, sometimes by cutting them out of the pregnant girl's body (also reported in Mozambique and Northern Uganda) or by banging them against trees or killing them with weapons. To survive, or because they hated babies conceived of rape, girls reportedly abandoned their babies by the roadside or left them at health clinics. Thus, being pregnant or the mother of children could have either highly adverse or relatively favourable consequences, depending upon the context and the girl's roles and status within a fighting force.

High numbers of maternal and child deaths were anecdotally reported in all three countries from causes other than direct violence. Dangerous childbirth practices were reported (some which pre-date the war), such as pushing on the pregnant girl's abdomen when labour contractions are strong and beating the mother when she is in labour and giving birth. Girls and women often gave birth alone. Abducted by RENAMO as a girl, Maria laboured alone, "I was pregnant when I was caught. I had to manage alone; no one helped me. It was not my first baby, so I had seen how to use the blade. I used the blade to cut the cord and then I just tied it" (Mozambique, interview, September 18, 2001). A midwife at Josina Machel Island who was working at a hospital when RENAMO attacked reported the following:

> I was with two pregnant women. We ran away and tried to hide somewhere. One of the women gave birth. We had to spend the night with the baby in our hands because we had no way to cut [the cord] until in the morning. The rebels blew out the back of the clinic (Mozambique, interview, September 19, 2001).

In Mozambique, leaves of a bean plant were put into the vagina to prevent pregnancy. Girls miscarried because of the harsh conditions within fighting forces—such as lack of food, water, and shelter and having to carry heavy loads or march long distances. Despite cultural, moral and legal prohibitions against abortions, they were reported in all three countries. Many girls died in the bush from forced or self-induced abortions. Abortions were induced by the girls themselves, and by nurses, doctors and traditional birth attendants who were taken into rebel forces. The most commonly reported method of inducing abortion was accomplished by using roots. Methods reported to be used by medical personnel were "shots" although the drug used was not named. A Ugandan nurse-midwife reported that, in Northern Uganda a vegetable and a local plant with oxytocic (uterine-contracting) properties were used ... "local herbs every little girl knows; because they are young, it is logical when they get that abortion in the jungle, most of them die. But a few lucky ones go through it. Many also have died in captivity because they only [have] those traditional birth attendants in the bush" (Uganda, interview, November 30, 2001).

Although preventing maternal and infant morbidity and mortality is extremely difficult, actions should be taken to minimize risk and restore normal reproductive functioning when girls return:

POLICY RECOMMENDATIONS
Governments, the United Nations, multilateral agencies and INGOs should

> Conduct epidemiologic studies in war-affected countries, in coordination with Ministries of Health, to improve knowledge of maternal, child and infant mortality, its incidence, causes and prevention.

> Develop, where possible, innovative ways to provide a minimal level of maternal child health care for girls in the bush. Safe Motherhood kits (to help prevent maternal and fetal infection and tetanus by providing soap, twine, a clean razor and a clean surface for birth) could be made available to all fighting factions.

5 Northern Uganda, Sierra Leone and Mozambique: Girls Entry and Experiences in Fighting Forces, Leaving the Forces and Disarmament, Demobilization and Reintegration

Northern Uganda (1987 to the Present)

This section, authored by Dyan Mazurana, presents country-specific findings and analysis regarding the presence, roles and experiences of girls and, to a lesser extent, young women, in Northern Uganda within the rebel Lord's Resistance Army (LRA). It also provides analysis about girls' experiences upon leaving the LRA (usually via escape or capture) and encounters with the government army, the United People's Defence Force (UPDF), rehabilitation centres established by national and international NGOs to assist returnees, and members of the various communities that they return to. It concludes with the girls' own analyses of their priorities for reintegration and rebuilding their lives and their perspectives on how the conflict in Northern Uganda can be resolved. The findings draw primarily on data collected in two studies, one conducted with Susan McKay and funded by CIDA in partnership with Rights & Democracy and the other conducted with Khristopher Carlson and funded by the Policy Commission of Women Waging Peace. By using quota sampling, Mazurana and Carlson were able to draw on in-depth work with 68 girls and young women in Northern Uganda to represent a population of 10,000 female ex-combatants/captives, accurate to plus or minus 12 percent (95 percent confidence interval).[8]

The Role of Gender in the LRA

FINDING:
Gender plays a central role in abduction and initiation into and training and duties within the LRA.

Most reports on girls within the LRA highlight their roles as sexual slaves and captive "wives" (see AI, 1997; Angulo, 2000; HRW, March and July 2003). Both Mazurana and McKay and Mazurana and Carlson found that girls' roles are divergent and complex. In Mazurana and Carlson's study population of former girl and young women captives within the LRA, the top three primary roles girls reported undertaking were as porters (41 percent), food producers (22 percent) and fighters (12 percent). However, of the study population, 49 percent reported that their secondary roles were as fighters, 72 percent reported receiving weapons and military training, and 8 percent received advanced military training. Interestingly, although discussions regarding the roles of girls within the LRA focus on them as captive "wives" only half (51 percent) reported serving as "wives" in either primary or secondary roles during their time in captivity.

---

8   See Appendix 1 for discussion of methodology.

A number of girls reported to both Mazurana and McKay and Mazurana and Carlson that nearly all girls taken by the LRA into Sudan receive military training (see also HRW, 1997) and that the LRA also abducts children from the Southern Sudanese populations, especially the Acholi, Dinka and Lukoya tribes. Rosa P., who was in the LRA from 1996–2002, reported that "[t]here were abducted Sudanese within the LRA the entire time I was with the LRA in Sudan... We would abduct the Dinkas and Lukoya children, make them carry heavy loads, sometimes kill them. We'd take young girls... as young as eight... they were used for fighting, most were killed in battle, they would be put in front" (Northern Uganda, interview, February 12, 2003).

Sudanese boys and girls are trained for combat along with abducted children from Northern Uganda. Both abducted Ugandan and Sudanese children and youth are divided among LRA commanders, and that commander then becomes responsible for their welfare. In turn, they provide free labour to the commander including, though not necessarily, sexual labour. Some abducted Sudanese girls are given to LRA commanders and fighters as "wives." Both girls and boys report that only commanders are allowed to have "wives," and boys who are common fighters are not allowed sexual access to girls or women. Boys interviewed by Mazurana and McKay report that girls who are "wives" of high commanders and those "wives" of commanders who are pregnant or have small children are given privileges, such as better access to food, medicines and looted goods (see also Muhumuza, nd).

Survivors reported to Mazurana and Carlson that the makeup of military training in Southern Sudan is largely consistent and begins upon arrival to a base location in Southern Sudan. All children and youth, except those females with very small children or who are pregnant, begin early every morning with forced singing and dancing at a frenzied pace. After hours of singing and dancing, at noon in the heat of the day the children are then forced to run in wide circles or up and down hills until the middle of the afternoon. Any boy or girl who drops from exhaustion is left to die; according to Joy P., "the weak ones would fall and die from thirst and hunger" (Northern Uganda, interview, February 13, 2003). In the middle of the afternoon, those who complete the running are given one plate of beans and one cup of water to share among seven to ten individuals, the only food and water given for the day. To supplement their diet, they forage and eat wild foods, leaves and grass. The training continues from one to three months. The majority of abductees die before or during the initial training period.

The boys and girls who survive the initial training are next given weapons training. Some reported being trained by Sudanese government forces during the mid- to late 1990s. Mazurana and McKay's and Mazurana and Carlson's informants also reported that the Sudanese government forces stayed in camps with or near the LRA camps (see also HRW, 1997). Some of the abducted Ugandan and Sudanese children would then be sent to fight Southern Sudanese populations, rebel forces, and/or the UPDF. Older boys were almost all sent to fight. Girls also participated in front-line combat. If a base was attacked in Southern Sudan or if the unit was attacked going into or while in Northern Uganda, all were expected to fight. Girls also held command positions within the LRA. According to Susan R., her unit, the Gilva Unit (which consisted of five smaller units), contained over 200 boys and 100 girls. Within the Gilva Unit, abducted girls served as captains, lieutenants and corporals. All girls in the unit were trained and expected to fight (Northern Uganda, interview, February 10, 2003). Another girl in the Gilva Unit, Mary O., was a commander. Mary hand-picked girls 15 and 16 years old to fight along with her. Of all the girls interviewed by Mazurana and McKay and Mazurana and Carlson, she was the only one released by the LRA after asking and being granted permission by LRA leader Joseph Kony; she had two children and had served for 12 years (Northern Uganda, interview, February 13, 2003).

Both Mazurana and McKay and Mazurana and Carlson found that girls performed support roles within the bases (see also AI, 1997; HRW, 1997; Isis, 2001a; Isis-WICCE, 2001b; Women's Commission, 2000). A number of girls reported that in the late 1990s when relations with the Sudanese government soured and they could no longer rely on them for food and supplies, until Operation Iron Fist (see also HRW, March and July 2003), their jobs were to raise crops or to make charcoal to sell in Juba; thus they were entering areas where UN and NGO staff would have potentially encountered them. Some crossed into Kenya to sell their goods and for trade. Others prepared food, carried loot, moved weapons and participated in raids on the Acholi, Dinka, and the Lukoya communities in Southern Sudan, stealing their food, livestock and seed stock, abducting their children and killing a number of civilians (see also Temmerman, 2001).

Any of the base occupants could be selected to fight if Kony's spirit told him they should go, including girls and young women who were pregnant or with children. Although usually exempt from fighting, in some cases, girls who were pregnant or had small children volunteered to fight as a means of attempting to escape. According to Ester R., mother of a 3-year-old child conceived and born in captivity, "I fought with my baby on my back. I asked to go, I asked for weapon. It was the only way [to] escape and I did, I escape" (Northern Uganda, interview, February 14, 2003).

Mazurana and McKay and Mazurana and Carlson found that some girls with several children who remained in the camps or moved with units attempted to escape; in some cases, they would take the smallest of the children and leave the others behind. Informants reported that other mothers within the camps, most often co-wives, would take on the role of caring for children left behind. Some informants reported to Mazurana and Carlson that with the increase of attacks due to Operation

Iron Fist, and with groups on the move, weapons were taken away from girls with babies or pregnant girls because of concerns that the girls might be more inclined to try to escape during an encounter with the UPDF. A number of informants who had been released by the LRA in June and July of 2002 reported that they carried weapons and were expected to fight until reaching the border of Northern Uganda, where their LRA commander collected their weapons from them. They then continued on with the rest of the group into Northern Uganda.

Ruth G. was interviewed one week after her escape. Because of Operation Iron Fist, she had moved with her commander-captor "husband" and his unit from Southern Sudan into Northern Uganda, at which time weapons were taken from the young women with children, including Ruth. During a UPDF helicopter gunship attack on her unit upon entering Uganda, she risked an escape. She told her oldest son, who was four, to hang on to her neck; she scooped her baby to her chest and carried a young boy of her good friend and co-wife on her back, "I could not leave the children with them [the LRA], so I took them all, even under these difficult conditions." Mazurana and Carlson asked Ruth what she would do now with the child of the co-wife, since she was without any material resources for herself or her own children. She replied that she would find a way to make do and raise the child as her own until the co-wife was able to escape and come for him. They had agreed to try to rescue each other's children if escape seemed possible. If the co-wife never came, she said she would raise the child as her own (Northern Uganda, interview, February 12, 2003).

A number of Mazurana and Carlson's informants who had escaped, been released by the LRA, or who had been captured or turned over to the UPDF noted that, because of the pressure exerted by Operation Iron Fist, the LRA was increasingly targeting girls for abduction. Girls and young women traditionally carry items on their heads and are accustomed to moving quickly with them. With Operation Iron Fist, the LRA was constantly on the move, and needed porters to move food and weapons. This practice of targeting girls was also reported to occur in the border region of Southern Sudan and Northern Uganda, with Sudanese girls abducted to serve as porters as the LRA moved back and forth across the border.

Estimates of Abducted Children

FINDING:
Considerable discrepancy exists among estimates of the number of abducted children in Northern Uganda, as well as of the number of returnee children who directly enter their communities and those who pass through reception or rehabilitation centres.

Widely varying estimates exist of abducted children in Northern Uganda (the districts of Gulu, Apac, Lira, Kitgum and Pader), as well as in the number of children returning and receiving treatment at the reception/rehabilitation centres for children and young adults associated with the fighting forces.[9] More abducted children and adults are likely to exist than has been acknowledged by the government of Uganda, the UN and international NGOs operating in the area. Beginning in June 2002 and continuing into 2004, abductions and insecurity in the North increased to such a point (see also HRW, March and July 2003) that current numbers of abducted individuals are extremely difficult to gauge. Thus, because all recent figures on abductees are gross estimates, the present situation provides an opportunity for UNICEF and other stakeholders to rework and refine their systems for collecting and managing data on abducted persons.

Additionally, it is generally believed that the vast majority of returnee children pass through one of the now five rehabilitation centres located in Northern Uganda that were established to assist children and youth abducted by the LRA (for example, Angulo, 2000; HRW, March and July 2003). Thus, although these centres are still significantly under-supported, especially since the tremendous increase in occupants over the past year, resources from donors and national and international NGOs have been consolidated in them. Yet, of Mazurana and Carlson's study population, 40 percent did not pass through any of the rehabilitation centres, and this figure likely represents a maximum threshold. Of girls who did not go through a reception or rehabilitation centre (N=27), 25 percent were never given the option, 21 percent said that no centres existed in their area, 18 percent did not know about such centres, 11 percent felt that the location of the centres was dangerous and therefore avoided them, and 7 percent wanted to go directly home. Girls' failure to enter rehabilitation centres cannot be primarily explained by proposing that they spent only a few days or weeks in captivity. The mean and median time in captivity of Mazurana and Carlson's study population was over four years, with some girls held for up to 12 years.

---

9 For example, UNICEF, which maintains the database on abducted children used by the Ugandan government and most international donors and NGOs, reports that 9818 children were abducted in Northern Uganda from 1990–2001. Of these, UNICEF notes that 4263 have returned and 5555 are still missing. Yet, of the five rehabilitation centres, the three most established centres for returnee children report different figures. World Vision reported approximately 5730 children passed through its centre by 2001; GUSCO reported that approximately 4370 children went through its program; and the KICWA assisted 578 children. Thus, the three centres saw approximately 10,678 children and adolescents by the end of 2001. This figure is 6415 more individuals than UNICEF recorded as having returned by the end of 2001.

Seventy-one percent of Mazurana and Carlson's study population went through the army barracks because they were captured by the UPDF or turned over by civilians or local government officials to the UPDF (see also HRW, March and July, 2003; Women's Commission, 2000). Of this sample (N=44), after leaving the barracks, 73 percent were sent to a rehabilitation centre, 25 percent went directly home or to find their (often displaced) parents, and 2 percent went to find a relative. Thus, 40 percent of the total study population and over a quarter of the sample who left the barracks received little or no medical, psychological or material support, which is provided by the rehabilitation centres. Importantly, the UPDF has been instructed to pass children through the UPDF Child Protection Unit (CPU), which is then to turn them over to the reception or rehabilitation centres or to civilian NGOs (Director of the CPU of the UPDF, Gulu District 4th Division Battalion interview, December 5, 2001; Sandra Oder interview, December 6, 2001). Yet, over a quarter of the sample was not taken to these institutions. Notably, all of the study population who had passed through the barracks did so after the CPU had been established.

POLICY RECOMMENDATIONS
The Ugandan government, the United Nations, donor governments and INGOs should

> Recognize that major differences in estimates of abducted and returning children reflect discrepancies in sampling, data collection and analyses and thus may misdirect the type and location of programmatic responses.

> Recognize that, while the Ugandan government has primary responsibility for the protection and welfare of its citizens, it repeatedly disregards the welfare of returnee children. The Ugandan government must intensify its efforts in these matters, and the international community must apply increased pressure on it to fulfill its obligations.

PROGRAM RECOMMENDATIONS
The Ugandan government, the United Nations, donor governments and INGOs should

> Recognize that because many girls enter communities without passing through reception or rehabilitation centres, resources need to be allocated to address their needs. Material, physical and emotional assistance for the girls and their families need to be built into and supported within the communities. In addition, resources and programs addressing the reintegration of girls who have passed through the centres should be strengthened.

Human Rights Protection

FINDING:
Protection of children's human rights is inadequate in the UPDF barracks.

Important gains have been made in sensitizing the UPDF to children's rights, particularly those of returnees or former LRA captives, and significant steps have been made with the establishment in 1999 of the UPDF CPU and its subsequent development. During armed encounters, the UPDF is at times instructed to fire in such a way as to disperse the children, instead of killing them, and to help enable their escape and capture. For example, if UPDF intelligence indicates that of a group of 50 LRA, perhaps only 20 would be armed, they would not use maximum force against the group (Director of the CPU of the UPDF, Gulu District 4th Division Battalion interview, December 5, 2001; Sandra Oder interview, December 6, 2001).

How often such tactics are used is unclear because captive children are injured and killed. Betty O., who was pregnant during her escape when her unit came under attack by a UPDF helicopter gunship, reported that her five-year-old son had been hit by a UPDF bomb during their escape and was wounded in the rib and back and now has no movement in his legs (Northern Uganda, interview, February 12, 2003). The two-and-a-half-year-old daughter of Innocence F., age 15, was shot by UPDF soldiers while she tried to flee from the LRA in September of 2002. She was unarmed and carrying her daughter when the child was shot. During their first night in the UPDF barracks, although badly wounded, her daughter did not receive any medical attention. They were held in the barracks for one month while her daughter's arm was treated prior to being released to a civilian rehabilitation centre. It is now scarred and deformed and the damage to the bone can be seen throughout its length (Northern Uganda, interview, February 12, 2003).

Before the development of the CPU within the UPDF, returnee children captured by or turned over to the UDPF commonly spent three to four months or longer in the barracks (see also HRW, March and July, 2003). The goal now, depending on their physical condition, is to transfer them within two weeks to NGOs for rehabilitative care (Director of the CPU of the UPDF, Gulu District 4th Division Battalion interview, December 5, 2001). Improvement in reducing the amount of time girls are held in the barracks is becoming more apparent. In Mazurana and Carlson's sample of girls who were held in the barracks (N=44), 75 percent reported being held from one to seven days, and 20 percent reported being held between two and four weeks. Important to note is that although girls are spending shorter periods in the barracks, not all are then transferred to rehabilitation centres.

In Mazurana and Carlson's sample of girls held in the barracks, 30 percent reported that they were well treated. For those who reported to have been treated well, most said that this came as a surprise, since they were told by LRA commanders that they would be immediately killed by UPDF soldiers if they were captured. When asked if anything was helpful during her time in the barracks, Grace P. replied "That we weren't killed. They gave us food and water, and no one touched us. We thought we would die, but no one touched us, we were well treated" (Northern Uganda, interview, February 13, 2003). Alice L. reported, "I was very afraid, I was sure I would be killed. But people welcomed us, gave us food. They said they were not going to hurt us, they want us all to come home" (Northern Uganda, interview, February 13, 2003).

While these reports represent positive and important developments, returnee girls and boys continue to face threats to their human rights while being held in UPDF barracks. In Mazurana and Carlson's sample of girls who had passed through the barracks, 23 percent reported fear of reprisals, lack of physical security and harassment by UPDF forces while there. Fama O., who left the barracks in July 2002, reported that some of the children held with her were so traumatized by their experiences in the LRA that they had stopped speaking. Fama reported that these children were beaten during interrogations to extract information and "to get them talking" (Northern Uganda, interview, February 14, 2002).

Some girls reported threats to their lives by UPDF soldiers while in the barracks, including assault and attempted murder (see also HRW, March and July 2003). Patience A. reported that she was being held in UPDF barracks in 2002 when the LRA carried out a particularly gruesome attack in which one member of the community was cooked alive and the others forced to eat the remains. The UPDF soldiers in her barracks were infuriated and dragged Patience out into the village where the attack had occurred, abusing her and saying that this is what people like her did, she deserved to die, and she should be killed right there. Patience said that it was only due to the intervention of a civilian man from the crowd that had gathered, who pleaded for her life, that they decided not to kill her and took her back to the barracks (Northern Uganda, interview, February 11, 2003). Lily P. said that during her time in the barracks in 2001 in Pader District, she was told that she should have remained a rebel "because she was a rebel" and the soldiers threatened to kill her (Northern Uganda, interview, February 17, 2003).

Some girls reported intense pressure to join the UPDF (see also HRW, March and July, 2003). Fama O. said that during her time in the barracks in July 2002 the UPDF would tell the children there that they would be re-abducted by the LRA if they went home so that those of them without children and who were older, around 15 years of age, should join the UPDF. "The soldiers should stop this and respect our dignity," Fama said, "...but quite a number of the children have joined" (Northern Uganda, interview, February 14, 2002).

At the same time, the UPDF reportedly continues to recruit children into Local Defence Units (LDUs). These militia forces are trained and supplied with weapons, uniforms, and salaries by the UPDF, making them for all practical purposes members of the UPDF.[10] Whereas they were supposed to be stationed in their home communities, some of Mazurana and Carlson's informants reported fighting against children their age in LDUs in Southern Sudan during Operation Iron Fist, indicating that they are being used as supplemental fighters outside of their home areas by UPDF forces (see also HRW, March, 2003).

Some girls reported lack of physical security in the barracks, including being left alone when the barracks came under attack by the LRA. Girls reported sexual harassment by UPDF soldiers and other LRA returnees. According to Robin K., some of the younger UPDF soldiers would become intoxicated and come into the barracks where the LRA girls were being held and harass them for sex. When Robin and some of other girls reported this behaviour to the barrack's officers, the officers harassed and beat them (Northern Uganda, interview, February 17, 2003).

Upon arrival at the barracks, children and youth from the LRA are to receive clothing, food, and, if necessary, medical attention (Director of the CPU of the UPDF, Gulu District 4th Division Battalion interview, December 5, 2001). Of Mazurana and Carlson's sample populations from the barracks, 55 percent reported that upon arrival at the barracks they did not receive clothing, 52 percent did not receive adequate hygienic materials, including soap and oil for hair and body, and 52 percent did not receive any medical attention, including some who were badly wounded or whose small children were shot or injured from bullets or shrapnel. These latter actions are in violation of international humanitarian law.

---

10 Northern Uganda, community leader interview, February 10, 2003; Northern Uganda, parents of abducted children interview, February 11, 2003; personal observation of local defence units in Gulu City, February 9; see also HRW, 2003.

POLICY RECOMMENDATIONS
The Ugandan government should
> Clarify and enforce policies prohibiting the recruitment of children into government armed forces, including the Local Defence Units.

> Conduct immediate investigations into gang-pressing and pressured recruitment of returnee children by the UPDF and move quickly to prosecute offending personnel.

> Ensure that if any UPDF barracks house children, they provide them with clothing, hygienic materials, including soap, oil and menstrual supplies, and immediate medical attention if necessary. Furthermore, ensure that girls and girl mothers and their children are housed under the direct supervision of females in separate locations from men and boys, as required under international humanitarian law.

> Ensure that children are transferred to Child Protection Units or civilian centres as soon as possible and when conditions allow for safe and secure transport.

> Immediately drop all charges of treason against child abductees and honour the amnesty granted to all ex-LRA child combatants and abductees.

The United Nations, governments and INGOs should
> Monitor and apply pressure on the Ugandan government to ensure that the above recommendations are carried out.

PROGRAM RECOMMENDATIONS
The Ugandan government should
> Strengthen the CPU of the UPDF to enhance its work and training in children's rights, with an emphasis on girls' rights.

The Ugandan government should
> Strengthen the work of local and international organizations that monitor the UPDF's treatment of children.

Rehabilitation Centres

FINDING:
Rehabilitation centres provide crucial services on-site, but face challenges with follow-up and reintegration.

Reception and rehabilitation centres provide crucial and reliable medical care, including mental health care, hygiene and material assistance for returnee children and adolescents (see also Women's Commission, 2000). When children arrive at a rehabilitation centre, such as GUSCO or World Vision, they are greeted by other children who clap and sing to welcome them. They are then given a basin for washing, new clothes and shoes, and some oil for their body and hair. They are bathed, have their fingernails trimmed, hair cut, and old clothes discarded to symbolize moving on to a new life. Several centres allow the children to undergo traditional healing or cleansing ceremonies, while others discourage this in preference to Christian religious ceremonies. The centres have nurses who provide routine nursing and health care for the children and youth and make contacts with hospitals for testing and additional medical care. The centres also employ counsellors and social workers who work with the children using a variety of approaches (see also Women's Commission, 2000).

In Mazurana and Carlson's sample of girls who passed through a reception or rehabilitation centre (N=41), 98 percent reported adequate physical, mental health, hygiene, and material assistance, and 80 percent rated their experiences in the centres as excellent or good.[11] Both Mazurana and McKay and Mazurana and Carlson found that girls who had passed through reception or rehabilitation centres stressed the importance of the care they were receiving in the centres and their perceptions were that they were well treated and respected (see also HRW, March and July 2003; Isis-WICCE, 2001a; Women's Commission, 2000).

During the late 1990s, the centres began to accelerate their work with communities where children were reintegrating and where community relations with the children were often severely damaged. Thus, healing those bonds represents a significant task.[12] Acceptance by the community is important for girls in rebuilding their lives. Although dedicated, the reception or rehabilitation centres are understaffed and under-funded relative to the magnitude of work need to carry out follow-up and reintegration work within the communities. Mazurana and Carlson found that follow-up by social workers when girls leave the centres is rare; of their sample of girls who passed through rehabilitation centres, only those living in the community and returning to the centre of their own volition reported receiving follow-up care by a social worker from a centre.

---

11 Some girls had already passed through the centres when Mazurana and Carlson interviewed them. To try to decrease levels of bias among those girls interviewed while still in the centres, the majority of the girls were interviewed by Mazurana or Carlson using an interpreter who had experience with girl captives but who was not a staff member of the facility.

12 Ochora Ochitti interview, November 30, 2001; Angelina Acheng Atyam interview, November 30, 2001; Josephine Amogm interview, December 4, 2001; see also Women's Commission, 2000.

Follow-up and reintegration assistance is needed, as returnee girls are often stigmatized and threatened when they attempt to reintegrate, including by husbands, immediate and extended family members, and community members (see also HRW, March, 2003; Isis-WICCE, 2001a, 2001b: Temmerman, 2001; Women's Commission, 2000). In Mazurana and Carlson's sample of girls who attempted to reintegrate (N=42), 64 percent reported feeling stigma, 41 percent reported being physically threatened, and 10 percent reported being physically attacked and beaten, with girl mothers reporting the highest rates of stigma, threat and abuse to themselves and their children. NGO policies of returning children to insecure environments in attempts to "reintegrate" them back into their communities are resulting in some re-abductions and killings of these children by the LRA.

Most girls who have escaped and are back in communities (i.e., not in barracks or centres), experience significant challenges because of insecurity and extreme deprivation (HRW, 2003; Isis-WICCE, 2001a; Isis-WICCE, 2001b: Temmerman, 2001; Women's Commission, 2000). In Mazurana and Carlson's sample of returnee girls living in communities (N=42), in response to an open-ended question about the greatest difficulties they were experiencing upon their return, half named material deprivation, including lack of food, 14 percent named emotional stress and stigma, 10 percent, fear of current insecurity, 10 percent, fear of past events, and the remaining percentage cited lack of school, medical care or housing, and loneliness.

In Mazurana and Carlson's sample of returnee girls living in communities, in response to an open-ended question about what was the most important factor in assisting their reintegration, 29 percent said nothing was helping. However, 20 percent named community support, 15 percent said family support, seven percent said counselling, while being in school, having access to skills training and prayer were all at five percent. Other answers including being in a secure place and having access to food. Thus, while community-based work regarding emotional acceptance and healing is crucial, it must be carried out in balance with material-based efforts to address the levels of deprivation and insecurity experienced by reintegrating girls.

POLICY RECOMMENDATIONS
The Ugandan government, the United Nations, donor governments and INGOs should

> Strengthen the work of the reception and rehabilitation centres to enable them to expand the on-site care they are providing and to assist the larger numbers of children now entering the centres.

> Make medical assistance available for returnees, including girl mothers and their children. Since many of the girls return directly to their communities, much of this assistance must be community-based.

PROGRAM RECOMMENDATIONS
The Ugandan government, the United Nations, donor governments and INGOs should

> Strengthen centres to expand upon the on-site care they give to returnees, with an emphasis on counselling and support to assist children in returning to school or entering skills-training programs.

> Strengthen centres to increase their outreach into communities, because many formerly-abducted children and adolescents are unaware of their existence. Children who have returned directly to their communities and later try to enter these centres should not be turned away.

> Strengthen community-based organizations to enable them to follow up and assist in promoting and upholding the reintegration rights of returning children. CPA Uganda is an example of a group carrying out this work.

> Create and standardize an effective procedure to assess risk of re-abduction after reintegration. When the risk of re-abduction is moderate to high, alternative plans should be available to returnee children until conditions allow for their return.

Schooling and Skills Training
FINDING:
Girls call for the right to education and skills training.

Most abducted girls, 87 percent in Mazurana and Carlson's study population (N=68), are taken during their primary school years; these findings are nearly identical to recent internal reports by UNICEF, Uganda (UNICEF, restricted internal document, January 2003). Even though primary schooling is free, many have not returned because their books and uniforms have been looted or destroyed, money is not available to replace them, schools are closed down because of rebel activity, or their families are displaced. In other cases, those who were in captivity for many years are ashamed to return to school and attend classes with younger children. Because of impoverishment caused by the war, few can afford secondary school (see also HRW, 2003: Isis-WICCE, 2001a; Women's Commission, 2000).

In Mazurana and Carlson's study population, whereas 43 percent had returned to school, 48 percent had not. Yet, 79 percent of Mazurana and Carlson's study population called for assistance to return to school, including the development of accelerated schooling (see also Women's Commission, 2000). "What I need you people to understand is I got to get to school," stressed 14-year-old Regina A. (Northern Uganda, interview, February 18, 2003). Regina and her 12-year-old sister were living as internally-displaced children in the town of Lira. Their father had been killed, Regina had been abducted and her mother had been injured during the attack on their village and was incapable of caring for the girls. The entire village had been abandoned, so when Regina escaped, she found her mother and sister living in Lira. As Regina explains, her problem is that there is no head of their household, she and her sister are children, their mother is weak, and they need to get back into school if they are going to be able to help themselves. Pauline A. is also looking for ways to re-enter school after being abducted from her Primary Four classroom, "I want to go as far as I can reach with my education" (Northern Uganda, interview, February 13, 2003).

Many girls are resourceful in coming up with coping mechanisms to find ways to stay in school. Fifteen-year-old returnee Grace F. is getting ready to enter Primary Six for the second time. Although she is one of the top students in her class, she does not have the resources to take the exams to pass into Primary Seven, or to pay for entering secondary school, so she continues to repeat Grade Six and is looking for ways to collect enough resources to eventually move on in her schooling (Northern Uganda, interview, February 17, 2003). Other girls who had been in the LRA for a number of years still wanted to return to school and suggested ideas for accelerated schooling. Models for accelerated schools now exist in Sierra Leone and the IRC plans to provide this type of schooling in Northern Uganda, with a $3 million grant from the US Department of Labor (DOL). It will target girls, including those with children.

A number of older girls and young women stressed the need for skills training; 75 percent of Mazurana and Carlson's study population identified skills training as a necessity in assisting them in reintegration (see also Women's Commission, 2000). At the same time, limited opportunities in skills training exist, with some skills markets so saturated (such as tailoring and carpentry) and the war's effects on the economy so detrimental that rehabilitation centres are currently considering offering different skills courses.

POLICY RECOMMENDATIONS
The Ugandan government, the United Nations, donor governments and INGOs should

> Support financially and promote girls' right to education.

> Support the development and implementation of accelerated schooling programs for older girls and boys who have missed out on several years of education. Programs developed in Sierra Leone by UNICEF and FAWE could serve as models

> Support market feasibility studies to help guide local and international NGOs working in Northern Uganda in the choice of marketable skills training they offer. Also, support the development and expansion of skills-training programs offered by some NGOs.

PROGRAM RECOMMENDATIONS
The Ugandan government, the United Nations, donor governments and INGOs should

> Support the education and skills-training programs of local schools and international and local NGOs working with returnee children. Educational programs developed by UNICEF, Sierra Leone, and the Forum for African Women Educationalists (FAWE), Sierra Leone, and skills-training programs developed by Caritas-Makeni, Sierra Leone, can serve as examples. In Uganda, examples include CPA, Uganda, WV, Gulu, and GUSCO, Gulu.

The Ugandan government should

> Provide protection to enable schools in the North to function and the pupils to remain free of abduction and attack.

> Offer free secondary education to children in the war-affected North, including school fees, uniforms and books.

Girl Mothers

FINDING:
Girl mothers face rejection and insecurity when attempting to reintegrate and confront significant obstacles in providing for themselves and their children.

"We return home, but to what?" (Northern Uganda, interview, November 20, 2001). Mazurana and Carlson's sample of formerly-abducted girl mothers (N=28) found a number of significant challenges upon return, including a lack of food and medicine for themselves and their children, little or no resources for their children, no means to provide for their children's schooling, high levels of rejection by former husbands, families, extended families and communities, and high levels of stigma, threat and abuse towards themselves and their children (see also HRW, 2003). A recent unpublished study by CPA, Uganda, reported similar findings (Dr. Frank Olyet interview, February 14, 2003).[13]

Agnes Y., a girl mother with two small children (ages one and two) conceived and born in captivity, said that due to insecurity in her village and the death of her parents, she is now living with a distant relative in Gulu City. The wife does not like her and treats her like a servant, routinely withholds food from her and her children,

---

13 Briefly, the CPA study worked with 59 girl mothers from five locations in Gulu District. Methods used to collect data included questionnaires, with a series of questions looking at problems of reintegration and coping mechanisms, relationships with community, family members and the girls' own children, and their future prospects. Interviews were conducted with the girls' parents, guardians and market vendors, to ascertain viable skills for them in future occupations, with NGOs encountering these girls and with local leaders. CPA was responsible for all data collection, management and analysis.

and is physically and verbally abusive. Agnes would like to leave but has no resources to shelter and feed herself and her children and does not know where other relatives are because they have been displaced (Northern Uganda, interview, February 11, 2003).

Notably, in Mazurana and Carlson's study population (N=68), 37 percent of the girls, including nearly all the girl mothers, were pregnant with children conceived in captivity. CPA's study found similar levels of pregnancy among their study population. Additionally, CPA reported that during interviews with parents or guardians of the girls, there were complaints of the girls going away with other men and returning later with more children and in need of more support. The parents identified their need for assistance and capacity-building to enable them to better assist their children and grandchildren (Dr. Frank Olyet interview, February 14, 2003).

Both Mazurana and Carlson and CPA's studies found that, in the reception and rehabilitation centres, although some of the children of girl mothers are of school age, activities or schooling are unavailable. Currently, the reception and rehabilitation centres are facing large increases in their populations and require more support to address the needs of all returnee children.

Both Mazurana and Carlson and CPA found that to minimize stigma, abuse and potential re-abduction, some girl mothers with their children prefer to live on their own in new communities or urban centres in the North. They have made deliberate choices to live away from their own communities and avoid living with other girl mothers for fear of drawing attention to themselves. They worry that if their presence is known, it might spark community abuse, as well as make them targets for re-abduction by the LRA. CPA's study found that the girl mothers did not trust each other and preferred to stay in isolation rather than being brought together.

Finally, both Mazurana and Carlson and CPA found that girl mothers placed high priority on the education of their children, often above their own access to it. Of Mazurana and Carlson's sample of girl mothers (N=28), 94 percent named access to education for their children as a top priority, although most had no means to send them to school. Mary A. said of her two-year-old daughter, "I am worried about schooling for my child, I want her to go to school" (Northern Uganda, interview, February 12, 2003). Innocence O., who was taken during Primary Three, spent eight years with the LRA, and returned with two children said, "My childhood is spoiled, my classmates are gone. If I could find a way to educate my children, maybe they will do what I could have done" (Northern Uganda, interview, February 13, 2003). Betty L., a mother of three children under the age of four who were conceived and born in captivity, stated, "Education for my children is important, it would give them hope in the future and maybe even a future for myself" (Northern Uganda, interview, February 18, 2003).

POLICY RECOMMENDATIONS
The Ugandan government, the United Nations, donor governments and INGOs should

> Recognize that approximately 30 percent of all returnee girls will be girl mothers, with higher numbers of girl mothers escaping in early 2003 or being released because of escalation in fighting.

> Recognize that rehabilitation centres are currently unable to provide assistance to the children of girl mothers for the duration of their stay, beyond basic materials, health care and food support. Strengthen financial support to these centres to enable assistance for children of girl mothers.

> Collaborate with the rehabilitation centres and girl mothers to develop programs to assist their children while they are in the centres and to begin or continue their schooling upon leaving the centres.

> Ensure that the rights of girl mothers and children born in captivity are clearly on the agendas in peace negotiations in both Sudan and Uganda. In particular, issues regarding the current lack of any national citizenship for children born in captivity in Southern Sudan must be addressed.

PROGRAM RECOMMENDATIONS
The Ugandan government, the United Nations, donor governments and INGOs should

> Collaborate with girl mothers to develop programs that include assistance with rent or simple housing materials, food, medicine and clothing for themselves and their children, access to education, skills training or income-generation programs.

> Provide childcare or access to school for school-age children while the young mothers attend school or learn a skill. Recognize that education programs should consider the rights and needs of girl mothers, in particular, by providing space and mats for their children and food for mother and child during the day.

> Develop programs to assist in the education of the children of girl mothers, because these young women possess limited ability or support to enable their children to attend school.

Dialogue for Peace

FINDING:

To achieve peace, girl and young woman returnees call for dialogue between the Ugandan government and the Lord's Resistance Army.

In Mazurana and Carlson's study population (N=68), 62 percent of girl and young woman returnees stated that the only way for peace to exist in Northern Uganda was for the government and the LRA to engage in dialogue, which should be aided by international intervention and mediation. In Mazurana and McKay's and Mazurana and Carlson's studies, informants stated that abducted children like themselves were being forced to fight against their will or to act as human shields (see also HRW, 2003; Isis-WICCE, 2001a, 2001b; Temmerman, 2001; Women's Commission, 2000). Ceasefires are continually broken by attacks by both the LRA and UPDF. A strong need exists for immediate international intervention to assist with a diplomatic solution to end the conflict and secure the release of thousands of captives.

POLICY RECOMMENDATIONS

The Ugandan government, the United Nations, donor governments and INGOs should

> Recognize that Operation Iron Fist has resulted in increased abductions in both Northern Uganda and Southern Sudan, in insecurity and death, and has failed to bring an end to the conflict.

> Utilize all good offices to support peace talks between the Ugandan government and the LRA to achieve a lasting peace.

> Urge the UN Secretary-General to appoint a Special Envoy to secure the release of captive children and adults held by the LRA and ensure a peaceful resolution to the conflict.

Sierra Leone

This section presents country-specific findings and analysis regarding the presence, roles and experiences of girls and, to a lesser extent, young women, in Sierra Leone within the rebel RUF, the rebel AFRC, the government SLA and pro-government CDFs during the 1991–2002 war. It then provides analysis about girls' experiences upon leaving the fighting forces and encounters with the official DDR process and interim care centres (ICCs) and rehabilitation centres established by national and international NGOs. It concludes with the girls' own analyses of their priorities for reintegration and rebuilding their lives.

Girls in Sierra Leone's Fighting Forces
FINDING:
Presence and roles of girls in all fighting forces are underestimated.

The estimated number of girls in fighting forces is higher than previously reported,[14] partly due to the presence of girls as full members of CDFs.[15] (Table 9). Girls and young women performed numerous roles within the fighting forces (see also AI, 2001; Coalition, 2001; HRW, 1998; HRW, 1999; Mazurana, McKay, Carlson and Kasper, 2002; Women's Commission, 2002). By using quota sampling, Mazurana and Carlson are were able to draw on in-depth work with 50 girls and young women in Sierra Leone to represent a population of 10,000 female ex-combatants/captives with accuracy equivalent to plus or minus 14 percent (95 percent confidence interval).[16]

---

[14] Force sizes are based on the most conservative and reliable estimates. Initial estimates generated by the UN and the government of Sierra Leone to prepare for DDR are not considered reliable as their estimates of total force populations were surpassed during actual DDR. Because of widespread blurring of roles of members of fighting forces (e.g., where porters and "wives" are also fighters), all members of the armed forces and groups are included within our estimates. Force estimates at the height of fighting for the RUF are 45,000 and for the AFRC, 10,000 (Radda Barnen, 2002). Force estimates of the AFRC at 10,000 seem highly improbable given that 8860 AFRC fighters passed through DDR (see Table 2). Based on the percentage of RUF personnel that passed through DDR (54 percent), likely AFRC force capacity was 20,000. Children constituted 50 percent of both the RUF and the AFRC (Radda Barnen, 2002), with girls comprising between 33 to 50 percent of those forces (Coalition, 2001; Radda Barnen, 2002). Mazurana and Carlson's field data confirm a high percentage of girls within the RUF and AFRC. The majority of females and males in the respective forces interviewed responded that children comprised approximately half of the RUF and AFRC forces in camps or compounds where they were held, and all reported the presence of girls in numbers equal to or slightly less than boys. Total force figures put the SLA at the height of fighting at approximately 14,000 fighters (Radda Barnen, 2002). Although the use of child soldiers by the SLA throughout the conflict is well documented, the percentage of children in the forces of the SLA is unclear. Based on UN reports we estimate 25 percent of some SLA/CDF forces were children (Coalition, 2001). Sources on the ground in Sierra Leone and Mazurana and Carlson's data gathered during fieldwork estimate that around 33 percent of the children in the SLA were girls and 10 percent of children in the CDFs were girls.

[15] It is widely argued that the CDFs were male-only secret societies that prohibited the presence of females or sexual contact with females. Our study documented women and girls serving as fully initiated members of two of the largest CDFs, the Kamajors and Gbethis, including as frontline fighters. Mazurana and Carlson conducted numerous interviews with women and girl CDFs themselves, male CDF fighters, those within the CDFs who initiated hundreds of women and girls, CDF commanders, RUF, AFRC, and SLA adult and child combatants who fought against them, civilians who saw them as fighters while in flight, and villagers who were protected by them. Because powerful members of the government of Sierra Leone denied the presence of children in CDFs, and because statutes in both the Special Court for Sierra Leone and the TRC deem the use of child soldiers as a crime, nearly all persons willing to discuss girls and women in CDFs did so on the condition of anonymity. Data regarding girls and young women in CDFs were collected in the Western District and the northern and eastern provinces.

[16] See Appendix 1 for methodology.

We found that most girls and young women reported that their primary roles were as cooks, fighters and domestic labourers, followed by porters, "wives" and food producers. Nearly half of the respondents received training from their commanders or captor-"husbands" in the use of weapons.

Table 9
Estimated Number of Total Forces, Children Associated with Fighting Forces and Girls in Fighting Forces

Force	Total Force	Total Number of Child Soldiers	Total Number of Girl Soldiers
RUF	45,000	22,500	7,500
AFRC	10,000	5,000	1,667
SLA	14,000	3,500	1,167
CDF	68,865	17,216	1,722
Total	137,865	48,216	12,056

Nearly all girls and young women in Mazurana and Carlson's study population performed additional secondary roles as cooks (72 percent), porters (68 percent), caring for the sick and wounded (62 percent), "wives" (60 percent), food producers (44 percent), messengers between rebel camps (40 percent), fighters (34 percent), spies (22 percent), communications (18 percent), and as labour in diamond mining for their commanders or captor-"husbands" (12 percent).

To illustrate, Mariama O. was captured when she was 11 by the RUF. She received military training and was selected to be a bodyguard of the senior commander and his captive "wife." She was trained in the use of and carried a two-pistol grip machine gun. The commander would move under her cover when he went out into the field and during fighting. She was also responsible for watching over the commander and his captive "wife" when back at the compound. Additionally, she served as a night security guard in the compound on alert for any attacks by CDFs or the SLA (Sierra Leone, interview, August 20, 2002).

"Wives" and fighters should not be viewed as exclusive categories (see also Mazurana, McKay, Carlson and Kasper, 2002; Sommers, 1997). For example, all respondents in Mazurana and Carlson's interviews who reported their primary role as fighters also said that they were forced to be "wives." Miata M., captured by the

RUF at age 12, was selected by one of the lower-ranking commanders to be his captive "wife" and shortly thereafter became pregnant. Even while she was pregnant, she was required to fight and did so up until her seventh month of pregnancy. Nurses who were captured by the RUF assisted Miata when she gave birth. After giving birth, she was held within the compound and performed domestic chores. Miata preferred being a fighter because it gave her greater access to looted items (including food), more chances of escaping, and if the compound was attacked she could better defend herself because she had a weapon (Sierra Leone, interview, August 20, 2002).

Gender and RUF compound structure: The RUF had a loose command structure, with individual senior commanders having significant influence upon the structure and tactics used for troops and captives. The RUF base structure was comprised of a compound with the senior commander and his "wives" heading the compound and the rest of the lower-ranking commanders, fighters and captives arranged into "family units" (see also Abdullah, 1998; Richards, 1996). Girls occasionally headed family units. Food and loot were distributed by the head of the unit; thus those not attached to a family unit were forced to live as scavengers. It was therefore to one's benefit to be part of a family unit; girls, at times, would use sex to bargain themselves into better positions within family units headed by kinder or more powerful commanders who had greater access to food and loot (Maurice Ellis interview, August 20, 2002; see also Sommers, 1997).

"Wives" of commanders held considerable power and influence within RUF compounds. When the commander was in the field or on mission, his captive "wife" or "wives" were in control of the compound. Most commanders' "wives" ranged in age from 9 to 19. In a commander's absence, his "wife" or "wives" would determine how looted items, including food, would be distributed. They were in charge of deciding whom from the compound to send on raiding, abduction and spying missions; they gave orders and enforced discipline in the camps; and some advised their "husbands" on military strategies. Commanders' "wives" had a series of armed bodyguards; most were older children who were selected by the commanders' "wives" because they were good fighters. Commanders' "wives" were also armed and trained in firearm use.[17]

The contrast in lifestyles for former RUF girls, especially "wives" of compound commanders who left high levels of material wealth (accumulated via looting), and returned at war's end to Sierra Leonean impoverished communities that were hard hit by the conflict has resulted in some girls feeling malcontent. In some cases, girls reported that life was better in the bush in captivity than the crushing poverty of home (Samuel Tamba Kamanda interview, August 29, 2002; Alfred Sesay interview, August 30, 2002).

---

17 Olayinka Laggah interview, August 13, 2002; four girl combatants' interview, August 20, 2002; four boy combatants' interview, August 20, 2002; two commanders' wives' interview, August 21, 2002; commander's wife interview, August 22, 2002; Glenis Taylor interview, August 27, 2002; Samuel Turner interview, September 4, 2002.

Captive-"wives" of commanders. Commanders' "wives" were, at times, in charge of small boy units (SBUs) and small girl units (SGUs). SBUs were made up of young boys aged six to 15 who were sent on numerous scouting and raiding missions and who were well known for the extreme violence they were forced to carry out against civilians, most notably amputations and dismemberment (AI, 2001; HRW, 1999; HRW, 1998; PHR, 2002; Richard Thoronka interview, August 23, 2002; Fatta Kamara interview, August 23, 2002; Philip Kamara interview, August 29, 2002). SGUs were made up of girls of a similar age and their primary tasks were information gathering and looting, although they also were forced to commit atrocities.[18]

In some cases, commanders' "wives" reported that they used loot to bribe or reward SBUs for not abusing young girls and young children within the compound (Sierra Leone, interview, August 22, 2002). In other cases, they could order punishment of SBUs for "disrupting life in the compound." Ruth B. said that the young children within the camps would, at times, accidentally discharge their weapons and kill other members in the compound. Other times, boys would kill each other over access to a particular girl. Such activities were punished by the commanders' "wives," and included severe beatings, being hung upside-down for long periods, being put into a deep pit for several days with little food or water, or being sent on food-finding missions, which were considered extremely dangerous (Sierra Leone, interview, August 21, 2003).

It was common for "wives" of senior RUF commanders to care for very young or particularly vulnerable children within the compound.[19] For example, Agnes D. was 14 years old, six months pregnant, and staying with her husband in Koidu when RUF forces attacked and she was abducted. She was taken with six other girls and young women to an RUF base; on the way, the group was attacked by SLA helicopter gunships, and all the other girls and women were killed. When she arrived, she was cared for by the wife of RUF leader Foday Sankoh. Since Foday Sankoh's group had been the one that abducted her, it fell to his wife to help care for Agnes (Sierra Leone, interview, August 20, 2002).

In some cases, as documented in Kono District, commanders' "wives" were replaced by more-favoured girls. Subsequently, the rejected "wives" were subject to serving as front-line fighters (Sierra Leone, two separate interviews, August 31, 2002). Ramatu S. and Inna T. were held in RUF camps in the south that separated captive civilians from fighters, to prevent civilians from reporting atrocities by particular fighters or relaying force strength to CDFs or the SLA should they escape. The girls reported that when "wives" of commanders or soldiers were rejected in favour of new girls, they were forbidden to return to the civilian camps, and were instead sent to the front lines (Sierra Leone, two separate interviews, August 31, 2002).

---

[18] Four separate anonymous interviews, August 21, 2002; anonymous interview, August 22, 2002.

[19] Four girl combatants' interview, August 20, 2002; four boy combatants' interview, August 20, 2002; two commanders' wives' interview, August 21, 2002; commander's wife interview, August 22, 2002.

POLICY RECOMMENDATIONS
The Sierra Leone government, the United Nations, donor governments and INGOs should

> Acknowledge that the presence, roles and experiences of girls within the fighting forces in Sierra Leone are more complex and multifaceted than previously reported.

> Recognize that captive "wives" of rebel RUF compound commanders held significant command and control power within rebel compounds. However, lack of recognition of this fact has resulted in operational and programmatic errors, including bias in the structuring and implementation of DDR and community-based reintegration and assistance programs (discussed in detail below).

> Re-evaluate these programs and develop supplemental programs for the majority of girls and young women who have been excluded.

Girls in CDFs
FINDING:
Girls and women were present as full members of CDFs.

Women and girls were fully initiated members of CDFs,[20] despite numerous claims to the contrary (Olayinka Laggah interview, August 13, 2002; see also for example Coalition, 2001, p.323, noting statements of (then) Sierra Leone Deputy Minister of Defence and National Coordinator of the CDF Samuel Hinga Norman). Mazurana and Carlson focused on the two largest CDFs, the Kamajors and Gbethis.

---

20 Francis Murray interview, August 15, 2002; Ibrahim Sesay interview, August 15, 2002; Ramatu Sama Kamara interview, August 21, 2002; anonymous interview, August 20, 2002; anonymous interview, August 28, 2002; anonymous interview, August 29, 2002; Binta Mansaray interview, August 30, 2002; anonymous interview, August 30, 2002; Shellac Davies interview, September 1, 2002; anonymous interview, September 2, 2002; Mr. Sylvester interview, September 3, 2002; four women leaders in village interview, September 3, 2002; two women leaders in village interview, September 3, 2002; anonymous interview, September 3, 2002; Alfred Lansana interview, September 4, 2002; Samuel Turner interview, September 4, 2002; two separate anonymous interviews, September 4, 2002; three separate anonymous interviews, September 5, 2002; Alfred Lansana interview, September 5, 2002; commander of Kamajors (name withheld) interview, September 5, 2002; anonymous interview, September 9, 2002; girl Kamajor interview, September 11, 2002; Michael Kamara interview, September 11, 2002; Samuel Kamara interview, September 11, 2002; girl Gbethis interview, September 12, 2002; Samuel Kamara interview, September 12, 2002, three separate interviews with three women Gbethis, September 12, 2002; Daniel Sahead Karoma interview, September 12, 2002; anonymous interview, September 12, 2002; girl Gbethis interview, September 13, 2002.

Although the Kamajors were originally a male-only traditional hunting society, in response to increased pressure from the RUF, beginning in the early 1990s and throughout the war, they became a self-defence force and enlisted women and girls. The Gbethis, never a traditional male society, were created as a CDF in the mid-1990s in response to increased rebel attacks. They modeled themselves after the Kamajors in a variety of ways, including particular rituals and fighting tactics. From their inception, the Gbethis initiated women and girls as fighters and in numerous other capacities within the fighting force.[21]

Initiation rituals were similar for both groups and consisted of being bathed with a mixture of native herbs by a spiritual leader within the fighting force (who, at times, was also a senior commander), the application of charms and the learning of taboos that if broken would render useless magical powers given to the person. Taboos were both ubiquitous, such as no pounding cassava at night, avoidance of particular kinds of foods (e.g., pumpkins and fried bananas), refraining from sexual intercourse without reapplication of herbs and charms, as well as unique to particular individuals, such as avoidance of being touched with a broom or touching the hand of a civilian. Rubbing of human blood on the newly initiated was done to give them a strong and fearless heart. Herbs and amulets were used to make bullets and pangas bounce off their skin. For those who desired additional powers, such as invisibility or shape-shifting, additional ceremonies, spiritual stages, and taboos were carried out or applied by the CDF spiritual leaders. If taboos were broken, most could be remedied by reapplication of herbs and charms.

With both the Kamajors and the Gbethis, women and girls were active throughout the war and served as initiators, commanders, spiritual leaders, frontline fighters, medics, herbalists, spies and cooks. For example, herbalists and cooks played central roles, since they were responsible for daily infusions of herbs into the meals of the members of the fighting forces to ensure their magical powers remained intact (Sierra Leone, two separate interviews, September 12, 2002). Such realities necessitate re-conceptualizing what the statement "the women just cooked" means within the Kamajors and Gbethis culture (a statement that was made repeatedly when Mazurana and Carlson inquired into the role of women and girls in CDFs).

---

21 Four women leaders in village interview, September 3, 2002; two women leaders in village interview, September 3, 2002; anonymous interview, September 3, 2002; Alfred Lansana interview, September 4, 2002; Samuel Turner interview, September 4, 2002; two separate anonymous interviews, September 4, 2002; three separate anonymous interviews, September 5, 2002; Alfred Lansana interview, September 5, 2002; commander of Kamajors interview, September 5, 2002; anonymous interview, September 9, 2002; girl Kamajor interview, September 11, 2002; Michael Kamara interview, September 11, 2002; Samuel Kamara interview, September 11, 2002; girl Gbethi interview, September 12, 2002; Samuel Kamara interview, September 12, 2002; three separate interviews with three women Gbethis, September 12, 2003; Daniel Sahead Karoma interview, September 12, 2002; anonymous interview, September 12, 2002; girl Gbethi interview, September 13, 2002.

Girls were fully initiated CDF fighters.[22] Amanda K. fought with 13-year-old girls in battles against the RUF in the North (Sierra Leone, interview, September 13, 2002). Some joined the CDFs at the request of their CDF husbands, others "joined" for reasons of survival or were abducted and forcibly conscripted by CDFs. Catherine L., a former Kamajor who "joined" at age eight and was a fighter, said that when RUF incursions increased, she looked for security for herself and her parents. "Being in love" with a Kamajor man was a method she used to seek additional protection (Sierra Leone, interview, September 11, 2002). Catherine also participated in abducting girls from villages during Kamajor raids; she and a group of ten girls would move through the villages on missions to abduct other girls and boys. She said that as the RUF would sweep through abducting many of the boys, the Kamajors would often target the remaining girls (Sierra Leone, interview, September 11, 2002). Mary P., a Gbethis, said that her group also targeted children, preferring "youths who had not a sexual life," as their power was stronger and purer (Sierra Leone, interview, September 12, 2002).

CDF girls and young women detailed widespread human rights violations by the CDF forces, including ritualistic murder (human sacrifice) and cannibalism of civilians within villages prior to attacks by CDF units against the RUF to ensure their invincibility.[23] For a number of reasons, including fear and resentment of CDF violence during the war, violation of gender roles and fear of magical powers, young women and girls formerly with CDFs described being stigmatized, threatened and abused upon returning to their communities.[24] For example, Ramata M. said that upon her return to her village she was punished and harassed by community members. She said that they were jealous of her power as a Gbethis and threatened to harm her to force her to leave the village she had helped to protect (Sierra Leone, interview, September 12, 2002).

---

22 Commander of Kamajors (name withheld) interview, September 5, 2002; anonymous interview September 9, 2002; girl Kamajor interview, September 11, 2002; Michael Kamara interview, September 11, 2002; Samuel Kamara interview, September 11, 2002; girl Gbethis interview, September 12, 2002; Samuel Kamara interview, September 12, 2002; three separate interviews with three women Gbethis, September 12, 2003; Daniel Sahead Karoma interview, September 12, 2002; anonymous interview, September 12, 2002; girl Gbethis interview, September 13, 2002.

23 Anonymous interview, September 11, 2002; two separate anonymous interviews, September 12, 2002.

24 Anonymous interview, September 11, 2002; two separate anonymous interviews, September 12, 2002.

POLICY RECOMMENDATIONS
The Sierra Leone government, the United Nations, donor governments and INGOs should

> Recognize that the presence of hundreds of girls and young women within CDFs requires that agencies rethink approaches for gathering information on children within fighting forces and subsequent programmatic responses. For example, in Sierra Leone, the presence of CDF girls was denied and they were therefore blocked from entering DDR.

> Recognize and address the fact that former CDF children and adolescents (at least in the two groups studied) were exposed to and participated in acts of extreme violence and human rights violations.

> Take gender-specific measures to counter the stigma, threat, and abuse CDF children and adolescents are facing within their communities.

Girls and Disarmament, Demobilization and Reintegration

FINDING:
Girl ex-combatants from all fighting forces were significantly underrepresented in DDR.

The *Lome Peace Accord* of 1999 set the framework for Sierra Leone's DDR program. Briefly, the DDR project was designed, funded and implemented by a number of national and international actors, including the government of Sierra Leone, the UN, the World Bank, donor governments and INGOs. The goals of the program were threefold: 1) to collect, register and destroy all conventional weapons turned in by combatants; 2) to demobilize approximately 45,000 combatants, 12 percent of whom were thought to be women, from the SLA, RUF, AFRC and CDFs, and; 3) to assist ex-combatants through demobilization to prepare them for reintegration. At its inception, Phase I was conducted by ECOMOG and the newly formed (1998) Sierra Leone NCDDR, chaired by President Kabbah. During Phase II, DDR was conducted by the UN Observer Mission to Sierra Leone (UNOMSIL) and NCDDR, and in Phase III by UNAMSIL and NCDDR (Malan, Meek, Thusi, Ginifer and Coker, 2003).

The DDR process: The combatant would voluntarily present himself or herself at a reception centre to disarm and surrender all weapons and ammunition. Reception centres were established in numerous locations throughout the country. A series of questions and performance of disassembly and reassembly of a gun, usually an AK-47, assessed combatant and eligibility status. Officially, those under 18 years of age were not required to present a weapon to enter DDR. Mazurana and Carlson found widespread discrepancy among UN and NCDDR officials and staff of NGOs working within the DDR process as to whether or not children had to turn over a weapon.[25]

---

25 Olayinka Laggah interview, August 13, 2002; Ibrahim Yoffendeh interview, August 15, 2002; Francis Murray interview, August 15, 2002; Cynthia Kallay interview, August 15, 2002; Maurice Ellis interview, August 22, 2002; Glenis Taylor interview, August 27, 2002.

Qualifying adults (18 years of age and over) were sent to a demobilization centre where they received a pre-discharge orientation, their benefits package and a small amount of resettlement and transportation money. Then they were discharged. Children (17 years and under) were sent to ICCs and then could select either skills training or an educational program of their choice. Such skills training or access to education is of paramount significance to many ex-combatants, since Sierra Leone is among the least developed countries in the world, its economy is war-ravaged, and most ex-combatants have few marketable skills and low levels of education, compounded by years of living in the bush.[26]

DDR participation: The DDR program in Sierra Leone is widely viewed as a success.[27] Overall, 92 percent of those who passed through DDR were males[28] (see Table 10).

Table 10
Participation in DDR in Sierra Leone by Force, Age and Gender

Force	Men in DDR	Boys in DDR	Women in DDR	Girls in DDR
RUF	16,735	3229	3925	436
AFRC	7,914	375	530	41
SLA	NA	445	NA	22
CDF	34,881	2003	296	7
Total	NA	6052	NA	506

---

26 Donald Robertshaw interview, August 12, 2002; unpublished statistical data provided to authors by United Nations Children's Fund (UNICEF), Sierra Leone, 2002; National Committee on Disarmament, Demobilization and Reintegration (NCDDR), Government of Sierra Leone, statistical data provided to authors by NCDDR, 2002.

27 Malan, Meek, Thusi, Ginifer and Coker, 2003; OCHA, February 24, 2003; OCHA, March 28, 2003.

28 NCDDR, Government of Sierra Leone, statistical data provided to authors by NCDDR, 2002; unpublished statistical data provided by UNICEF, Sierra Leone, 2002.

Based on data presented in Table 9 (Estimated Number of Total Forces, Children Associated with Fighting Forces and Girls in Fighting Forces), Mazurana and Carlson drew on UNICEF, Sierra Leone, and the Sierra Leone NCDDR data (unpublished statistical data provided by NCDDR, Government of Sierra Leone, 2002; unpublished statistical data provided by UNICEF, Sierra Leone, 2002) on overall force participation and girls' participation in DDR (Table 11).

Table 11
Girl Combatants and Their Presence in DDR Programs in Sierra Leone

Force	No. of Girls in Force	Girls in DDR	% of Total Force in DDR	% of Girls in DDR
RUF	7,500	436	54 %	6 %
AFRC	1,667	41	89 %	2 %
SLA	1,167	22	No data	2 %
CDF	1,722	7	54 %	0.4 %
Total	12,056	506	NA	NA

Substantial disparity exists between the numbers of girls within the forces and those entering DDR programs, thus calling into question the design, implementation and success of these programs.

While, officially, children were not required to present a weapon to enter DDR, both Mazurana and McKay and Mazurana and Carlson found a widespread perception among the girls and young women that a weapon was required for entry into DDR. For example, in Mazurana and Carlson's sample of those who did not go through DDR (N=25), 46 percent cited not having a weapon that was required for entry. Additionally, according to nearly all respondents who passed through DDR, the weapons test with an AK-47 was repeatedly administered to children to determine their admission into programs (Sierra Leone, interview, August 29, 2002; Komba Boima interview, September 2, 2002; see also Women's Commission, 2002). One hundred percent of Mazurana and Carlson's study population who entered DDR (N=25) were asked to turn in a weapon and perform the weapons test.

Notably, although Phase I and Phase II required all participants to produce a weapon for entrance, Phase III allowed for group disarmament, in which a group could disarm with heavy weapons or a number of weapons or ammunition. It was believed that this would allow for greater participation of women and girls (Olayinka Laggah interview, August 13, 2002). However, while total numbers of all participants increased in Phase III, proportions of women and girls did not markedly increase: in Phase I, girls and women accounted for approximately 6 percent each of disarmament totals; in Phase II, women were at 6 percent and girls at .06 percent, and in Phase III, women were at 7 percent and girls were .07 percent (unpublished statistical data provided by NCDDR, Government of Sierra Leone, 2002; unpublished statistical data provided by UNICEF, Sierra Leone, 2002).

Insecurity and Violence at DDR Sites: Insecurity and fear of violence were also key factors in girls and young women avoiding or leaving disarmament and demobilization sites early (see also Women's Commission, 2002). For example, in Mazurana and Carlson's sample of those who did not enter DDR, 21 percent cited fear of reprisals and insecurity at the centres. Those girls and young women who did enter DDR noted that disarmament and demobilization sites were full of adult males, crowded, and lacked proper security and hygienic and medical care. Helen O., a former CDF, said she left the demobilization site after a few days because of the sleeping conditions. She said the site was overcrowded with large numbers of men and, as a female, she feared for her safety (Sierra Leone, interview, September 12, 2002). Insecurity in ICCs was also a problem noted by girls in CDFs, who reported that they were interviewed by staff about their force affiliation in locations where other children were present. The majority of children in the ICCs came from the RUF; when they learned that a CDF child was present, threats to the security of that CDF child by former RUF fighters would occur as soon as the child left the interview. This caused some study respondents to leave the centres within a few hours, fearing for their lives (Sierra Leone, interview, September 11, 2002).

Additionally, for girls and young women in the CDFs, the fact that they are female, and the belief that females did not exist in these groups, was used as justification to prevent the vast majority from entering DDR programs (Olayinka Laggah interview, August 13, 2002; Sierra Leone, interview, August 22, 2002). A senior CDF commander in the North reported that he was told by the government and UN peacekeeping forces to organize his forces (of over 2000) in his village and the government and UN vehicles would come and take them to disarm. He gathered his troops, but only the men and boys were taken, leaving behind around 500 women and girls who were fully initiated CDFs. When he asked why they had left the women and girls, they informed him that females were not part of CDFs (CDF senior commander and initiator [29] interview, September 12, 2002).

Finally, classification of women and girls abducted by the RUF, AFRC and SLA into the near-exclusive categories of "sex-slaves," "wives" and "camp-followers" prevented the establishment of DDR programs that addressed the experiences of many girls and young women, since these groups were to be excluded from formal entry into DDR (Olayinka Laggah interview, August 13, 2002). Programs for "wives" were belatedly established to address the fact that male ex-combatants were running out of money given to them from DDR and were coming back and demanding that NCDDR officials assist them. One response was a program that enabled "wives" of male ex-combatants to qualify for micro-credit to help enable sustainable activities for the family. However, to qualify for the program, the girl or woman had to be accompanied by the male ex-combatant who would vouch she was his "wife"—these girls and women could not come forward on their own to claim benefits. This resulted in some men abducting girls and women to pose as their "wives," collecting their money, and abandoning them. Additionally, since economic factors play a primary role in girls and women remaining with captor-"husbands," especially girl mothers, such programs may have inadvertently contributed to girls and women remaining in violating relationships.[30]

POLICY RECOMMENDATIONS
The Sierra Leone government, the United Nations, donor governments and INGOs should

> Recognize that bias in design and implementation of DDR programs resulted in girls' near exclusion from DDR programs and benefits. Girls within the SLA and CDFs were particularly marginalized. While the efforts of child protection agencies operating in Sierra Leone are among the best to date, because of gender biases within the DDR program, alternative approaches should be sought to address the needs and rights of the many girls excluded from the programs, potentially under the umbrella of war-affected children.

---

29 Initiators are persons who perform rituals to initiate others into CDFs, usually through ceremonies that impart magical powers to protect the person during battle. These people are considered to have great magical and physical strength.

30 Olayinka Laggah interview, August 13, 2002; Samuel Tamba Kamanda interview, IRC, August 22, 2002; anonymous interview, August 31, 2002. Violating relationships are those in which girls and women's dignity and human rights are violated by their partners, spouses or family members.

> Assess the situation of children from the various fighting factions and develop specific objectives, strategies and activities that respond to their particular experiences and needs. Do not assume that all children participating in and among fighting forces have similar experiences or needs.

> Recognize that disarmament and demobilization camps were constructed to attract large numbers of male fighters and adequate attention was not given to mechanisms to ensure the protection of women and girl combatants and to uphold their human rights.

> Ensure that centres for children and young mothers are established early in the DDR process and that adult female staff is present.

The United Nations, governments and INGOs should

> Acknowledge that requirements of weapon possession and functional knowledge as a "ticket" into DDR blocks the entry of many girls and young women and should be avoided as a requirement for children and youth in all future DDR programs. Work to ensure clarity and consistency in not requiring children to produce weapons or perform weapons tests to enter programs.

> Take measures to ensure that future camps and sites are designed in ways to protect the rights of all ex-combatants, especially girls.

PROGRAM RECOMMENDATIONS
The Sierra Leone government, the United Nations, donor governments and INGOs should

> Work in conjunction with UNICEF, Sierra Leone, to support research into the location, numbers and assistance needs of girls and young women associated with fighting forces who were excluded from entering DDR. In particular, the research should seek out and assess the situation and needs of girls and young women formerly with CDFs.

> Work in close partnership with UNICEF, Sierra Leone, to support educational and skills-training programs to address the needs of girls and boys associated with CDFs and the SLA. Additionally, community mediation programs regarding children associated with CDFs should be developed and supported. Caritas-Makeni is a local NGO with such programs.

FINDING:
Girls' rights fall short in DDR.

Girls did not routinely receive appropriate care, gender-specific or otherwise, during DDR (see also Women's Commission, 2002). Fifty percent of Mazurana and Carlson's study population (N=25) entered the official DDR process. With regard to materials available at the ICCs where persons 17 years of age and under were taken and demobilization centres where persons 18 years of age and older were taken, 43 percent of girls and young women reported not receiving adequate clothing; 54 percent reported a lack of proper hygiene materials, including soap, shampoo and menstrual supplies; and 23 percent reported they did not have access to medical care when requested. It was policy that all children entering ICCs were to receive basic materials, which included sandals, sleeping mats, blankets, used clothing and soap, in addition to two meals a day and access to counselling. It was reported that a number of children sold the goods they received, or stole them from other children and sold them for cigarettes or candy (Donald Robertshaw, personal communication, March 25, 2002). However, it also appears that UNICEF and the implementing NGOs experienced supply problems. Some ICCs did not provide routine medical screening for ex-combatant children. In comparison to the rest of the study population, young women respondents reported the poorest physical and safety conditions at adult demobilization centres.

The majority of Mazurana and Carlson's sample (N=25), 35 percent, stayed in the ICC one to seven days, 27 percent stayed two weeks to a month, 18 percent stayed one to three months, and the remainder stayed six months or more. Fifty-six percent reported they had not received the monetary benefits they were promised in demobilization. This is a leading factor in rising tension among child ex-combatants, resulting in rioting, strikes and attacks against NGO staff and property.

Thus, while the DDR program in Sierra Leone has made important strides regarding the treatment of child combatants and those associated with fighting forces, programs in locations such as Angola and the Democratic Republic of Congo need to improve their ability to address the situation of girls in these fighting forces.

POLICY RECOMMENDATIONS
The Sierra Leone government, the United Nations, donor governments and INGOs should

> Review and strengthen policies and procedures for ensuring adequate hygiene, clothing and medical supplies for child ex-combatants and identify gaps. Reasons for abbreviated lengths of stay at ICCs should be analyzed, with a focus on gender, protection and human rights issues. Results and lessons should be used by agencies to inform current child demobilization programs underway in other countries, such as Angola and the Democratic Republic of Congo.

> Recognize that failure by the government to pay benefits to child combatants causes particular hardships for girl mothers. At times, this has led the girls to resort to violent means of protest and has resulted in increased insecurity for government, UN and NGO staff working with child ex-combatants.

Girls, Skills Training and Education
FINDING:
Girls cite access to skills training and education as the most important factor in assisting their reintegration.

In Mazurana and Carlson's study population (N=50), 50 percent of the girls and young women surveyed named material deprivation, including lack of food, clothing and housing, as the greatest challenges to their reintegration. Forty-nine percent of respondents said participation in skills training was the most important factor in mitigating the hardest aspects of reintegration (for similar findings, see also Women's Commission, 2002). Ninety percent of the study population reported that the training was or would be important for them and rated it as excellent or good. However, some girl mothers are unable to attend skills-training classes, for example, because they lack adequate child care, which, in their cases, was related to stigmatization and rejection by their families who might welcome the girls back, but not their children.

Seventy-five percent of Mazurana and Carlson's study population expressed a desire to return to school and to become literate. Thirty-eight percent of the study population had received some schooling prior to, during or after the war. Of those, 84 percent had been in school prior to entry into the fighting forces. Yet, only 11 percent of them had been able to return to school after the war and only two new students enrolled.

POLICY RECOMMENDATIONS
The Sierra Leone government, the United Nations, donor governments and INGOs should

> Recognize that access to skills training and education is a key factor in assisting girls' reintegration. However, most girls in the fighting forces did not qualify for DDR and thus are not benefiting from these programs. Efforts should be redirected at the community level to assist girls in returning to school or entering skills training. The current efforts of UNICEF and the United States Agency for International Development to provide funding and services (e.g., skills training, health education, literacy, day care and formal education) for girls and young women who did not pass through DDR are examples of such programming.

> Encourage and support local and international NGOs to address the rights and needs of girls in the fighting forces within their programs. Work together to identify and address the reasons why the numbers of these girls in school are significantly lower than boys.

PROGRAM RECOMMENDATIONS
The Sierra Leone government, the United Nations, donor governments and INGOs should

> Assist in the development and support of income-generating skills training and educational programs for children associated with fighting forces, in particular, girls and girl mothers. Examples of such programs are the Caritas-Makeni programs located in Port Loko, Mile 91, and Makeni.

> Ensure that skills training includes basic literacy and numerical skills to help girls manage future accounting. Examples of such programs for girls and girl mothers are Caritas-Makeni in Port Loko and Makeni.

> Recognize that skills-training programs should consider the rights and needs of girl mothers, in particular, by providing space and mats for their children and food for mother and child during the day. Similar considerations should be taken into account for girl mothers who wish to return to school. Because of stigma and rejection, relying on family members to take care of the children of girl mothers during the day does not appear to be realistic, and other means should be developed.

> Develop and strengthen access to schooling, including accelerated schooling, for older girls and girl mothers. Examples of related programming include UNICEF, Sierra Leone, and FAWE, which enable communities to benefit from ex-combatant children returning to school and their accelerated schooling programs.

Mozambique

This section presents country-specific findings and analysis regarding the presence, roles and experiences of girls and, to a lesser extent, young women, in Mozambique within the government FRELIMO and rebel RENAMO forces during the 1976–1992 civil war. It also provides analysis about girls' experiences of joining and abduction into these forces, the multiple roles they played, their experiences of DDR, and challenges they face in the post-war period. The findings presented here draw primarily on data collected with Susan McKay in the CIDA/Rights & Democracy study.

Presence and Roles
FINDING:
The presence and roles of girls in fighting forces are more prevalent than reported.

Throughout the civil war in Mozambique (1976–1992), young women and girls were involved in fighting forces with the government forces of FRELIMO and the rebel group of RENAMO. RENAMO made greater use of children in its forces than did FRELIMO (Efraime and Errante, nd; HRW, 1992; Manning, 1998). Based on demobilization data we collected from AMODEG on 482 female ex-combatants, in total, 36 percent entered the armed forces at age 17 or younger, with 17 percent entering FRELIMO and 82 percent entering RENAMO at age 17 or younger.

Recruitment: In 1975, FRELIMO began recruiting and gang-pressing girls into their forces for the war against RENAMO. Anna R. joined FRELIMO as a girl because its gender-equitable propaganda promised new and emancipatory roles for women. Upon her arrival at the base, however, she found little room for personal development under a strict command structure (Mozambique, interview, October 2, 2001). Other respondents joined to escape rural areas, to improve education and career opportunities, and to expand gender roles. Some were gang-pressed. For example, beginning in 1975, FRELIMO recruiters with buses arrived at schools and asked girls to volunteer for the military; when few volunteered, a number of girls were rounded up and forced onto the buses, despite protests from the teachers and the girls. This process was repeated at a number of schools until the buses were full. The girls were then brought to and held at the Mowamba military base, where they waited until the number of girls brought there reached 500, at which time their military training began (Mozambique, two separate interviews, October 2, 2001).

Girls were also active in RENAMO forces. While much has been written about adults and children being abducted into RENAMO (HRW, 1992; Vines, 1991; Wilson, 1992), we found that nine years after the war, some people appeared more inclined to report dissatisfaction with the FRELIMO government and their own active involvement in seeking out and joining RENAMO; previously, most people reported they were abducted into RENAMO (see for example HRW, 1992; Wilson, 1992). Some girls joined RENAMO because of discontent over FRELIMO's socialist policies, which included benefits to particular regional and ethnic groups, primarily in the south, land reforms, consolidation of farming land and labour, and undermining of traditional forms of authority (Chingono, 1996). Carolyn B. explained why she joined RENAMO as a girl,

> People were living under harsh conditions, no food. They have to fetch for everything, even [if] food in store nobody has money... the RENAMO say that all this would be over, okay. People would be free. People would have everything they need and they would handle the socialists and the country would be changed. So that is why I went with the RENAMO... I can see that because I saw my parents suffering to feed us, going to the fields to find everything, sugar, rice. So it wasn't life for human beings. So I wanted to find something different (Mozambique, interview, October 2, 2001).

Working underground, RENAMO established ties with sympathetic community and traditional leaders, who would then take interested recruits to meet RENAMO recruiters (see also Chingono, 1996; Manning, 1998). Several of our informants came to RENAMO this way and were accepted into the force after explaining their reasons for wanting to join (Mozambique, interview, October 2, 2001). Some joined with family members, mostly fathers, brothers or uncles, who were involved with RENAMO (Mozambique, interview, October 1, 2001). Others joined because of lack of educational opportunities under the FRELIMO government. Some of these girls were recruited as part of RENAMO's campaign of promising students education opportunities abroad (Manning, 1998), which, for our informants, never materialized. Instead, upon arrival at a RENAMO base, they were told they would not receive an education, but were now members of the RENAMO force and could not return home (Mozambique, interview, October 1, 2001; see also Manning, 1998).

Abduction: Girls were also abducted into RENAMO forces (Chingono, 1996; Efraime and Errante, nd; HRW, 1992; Vines, 1991; Wilson, 1992). A religious leader in an area that saw heavy fighting throughout the war explained,

> The women suffered a lot during the war. Every night we had to hide in the bush, the women and girls hid, even so, the bandits [RENAMO] would find them, take them to the bases and rape them. The women [and girls] were also forced to carry things. When the bandits take a girl to a base, and they come and take

more girls, and keep taking girls, products, food, cows, and burned our houses. They would take even babies and young boys as soldiers (Mozambique, interview, September 18, 2001).

Although most international agencies did not recognize the fact that significant numbers of girls were involved in both fighting forces, it was common knowledge among Mozambicans. Agostinho Mamabe, now head of a national NGO in Mozambique, worked with children during the war and in its immediate aftermath. In commenting on the exclusion of girls and young women associated with the fighting forces from the planning processes of the UN and INGOs, Mamabe explained,

In Mozambique we had a different situation, girls here had to go to the Army, [they were] called girls' department or girls' groups from the arbitrators. [Thus,] specifically in Mozambique we were concerned about this, because the government did not make any difference between men and girls to go to the Army... So for a certain number of years, we had girls going regularly to the Army. But at the time we talk[ed] about the demobilization in this country, no one talked about that—just [they talked about the] men. And I think the UN had strong, strong power on making the decisions there also. [Because it was common knowledge that girls were involved on both sides] I would see us extremely normal that we talked about girls, and I wonder why we didn't talk about it. I know that in RENAMO there are cases of girls who are even commanders (Agostinho Mamabe interview, September 12, 2001).

Roles: Girl ex-combatants from FRELIMO and RENAMO performed a variety of roles, such as fighters, trainers for incoming recruits, intelligence officers, spies, recruiters, medics, first aid technicians, weapons experts, slave and domestic labour, and captive "wives." Maria F. joined FRELIMO when she was 17 years old and eventually became a captain. "I never forget that during the war we [were] trained how to use guns. I know how to cock the gun. I know everything about guns" (Mozambique, interview, September 26, 2001). At age 15, Banda Z. joined FRELIMO and received military training. At age 17, she became a tactics instructor, training both males and females in military tactics, use of small arms and light weapons, laying ambushes and map reading (Mozambique, interview, October 1, 2001).

Juliane D. joined RENAMO on the promise of a scholarship to study abroad that never materialized. Literate in a number of languages, including Portuguese, she was soon made part of the RENAMO senior intelligence department that reported directly to the President of RENAMO. This intelligence department was primarily made up of students like herself; she reported that there were over 100 intelligence officers, all of them youth and 10 percent of them girls (Mozambique, interview, September 27, 2001; Joao Candido Pereira interview, October 3, 2001).

Patterns of recruitment and abduction of girls and young women revealed RENAMO's and FRELIMO's changing military and political needs. Our informants who were with RENAMO fighting forces said that upon abducting groups of children and adults, RENAMO would routinely ask their education or training levels; those who were illiterate tended to be used as slave labour, frontline fighters and given to soldiers as rewards or captive "wives." Those who were educated or had some skills training considered themselves "lucky" as they were put into positions or given training where their skills could be used, such as medics or intelligence officers. Thus, conditions for them were not as brutal as for the illiterate rural residents, who were abducted to serve as slave labour. As the war progressed and RENAMO realized that it had to turn itself into a political party to survive the end of the war, it began heavily recruiting students into its ranks (Manning, 1998), including girls. As FRELIMO saw the war coming to an end, it also began reorganizing its force structure by allowing women who had joined as girls to leave the force or forcing them out of positions they later gave to male fighters (Mozambique, interview, September 26, 2001; Mozambique, interview, October 1, 2001).

When the war ended, some of our informants chose not to return to the rural communities they had lived in prior to being abducted into or joining the fighting force, preferring to stay in urban centres. They felt this would provide them and their children with additional opportunities, which for many did not materialize (Mozambique, interview, September 26, 2001). Additionally, some noted that by staying in an urban setting they would be able to be in contact with other girls and women who had had similar experiences, "[We] don't want to move out [of the cities]. [We] are not alone here" (Mozambique, interview, September 26, 2001).

POLICY RECOMMENDATIONS
The Mozambique government, the United Nations, donor governments and INGOs should

> Recognize that the participation of girls and young women in the war in Mozambique was much more widespread than previously thought.

> Recognize and address the fact that policy and programs to assist in post-conflict reconstruction reflected the absence of attention to the gender-based needs or experiences of girls and young women associated with fighting forces.

> Support the work of international and local NGOs working among war-affected communities, with particular attention to gender-aware and women-empowering programs.

Girls and DDR
FINDING:
UN and government DDR programs at the end of the war privileged male combatants at the expense of women and girls, whose loss of educational and marketable job skills due to time spent in fighting forces and little to no government assistance for female ex-combatants contributed to long-term, post-conflict cycles of poverty.

"Basically when we talk about girls and demobilization, we are talking about something that never happened," (Agostinho Mamabe interview, September 12, 2001). Few former female ex-combatants passed through Mozambique's DDR or received benefits. Most received no assistance from the government, then or now. Notably, a number of former FRELIMO combatants attributed their exclusion to the fact that the government did not want to admit or have evidence generated regarding their use of girls. Speaking about the DDR process, Mamabe explained that most DDR programs are set up as a bridge between military and civilian life for soldiers, which he argued is a mistake, as there are numerous other groups associated with the fighting forces that are also in need of demobilization, such as girls and boys (Agostinho Mamabe interview, September 12, 2001).

Camp composition and long periods of time spent in demobilization camps also contributed to women and girls' low participation in DDR. At one point in the DDR process, women ex-combatants with children were asked to gather to receive payments and assistance; they gathered, they waited, but there was no money and no assistance given (Mozambique, interview, September 26, 2001). In some cases, ex-combatants stayed from several months to three years at UN assembly points awaiting benefits, during which time some young women, in particular those with children, left due to economic inability to support their children and insecurity in the camps (Agostinho Mamabe interview, September 9, 2001; Mozambique, two separate interviews, October 1, 2001).

Violations of young women and girls' human rights occurred within the camps, in particular, regarding fights between captor-"husbands" and original husbands, fathers or brothers trying to secure release of captive females. Usually the soldiers, who often maintained possession of their weapons, were victorious (Agostinho Mamabe interview, September 9, 2001; Abu Sultan interview, October 3, 2001).

Some young women and girls were forced to accompany their captors during resettlement, while others were left on the side of the road, at times with their children (Abu Sultan interview, October 3, 2001; see also Thompson, 1999).

Due to length of time in service, both RENAMO and FRELIMO ex-combatants have lost educational and skills-training opportunities. Consequent lack of adequate employment directly contributes to their inability to send their own children to school, thus continuing the cycle of poverty. Anna R. explained, "We all have children and they can go to school until one level [but it is] not possible to continue because of the cost of the school... So how to get them in this level when we don't have money, we don't have nothing... That's our trouble, it is very, very hard" (Mozambique, interview, September 26, 2001).

POLICY RECOMMENDATIONS

The Mozambique government, the United Nations, donor governments and INGOs should

> Recognize that bias, lengthy demobilization processes and poor camp design contributed to most young women and girls not officially demobilizing. Others left before they collected their benefits because of economic hardship and insecurity in the demobilization camps.

> Recognize and address the fact that length of stay in the fighting forces has meant that some young women and girls have lost education and job opportunities. The majority left the forces with no compensation, few marketable skills and little means to support themselves and their children. This directly contributes to being unable to send their children to school, thus continuing cycles of poverty and human insecurity.

Cross-cutting Findings

This section includes key cross-cutting findings from country-specific research in Northern Uganda, Sierra Leone and Mozambique.

Concealing Girls' Involvement
FINDING:
Governments conceal the use of girls in their own fighting forces, while highlighting their presence in opposition forces

The use of girls and boys by rebel or opposition forces is well known (see for example Coalition, 2001). Significantly, we found that governments are complicit in abducting, gang-pressing, and recruiting girl and boy combatants to fight armed opposition groups that also use child combatants. These governments use the high visibility and international outrage over "child soldiers" to highlight the brutality and illegitimacy of the armed opposition's use of children, thus using the girls and boys as political pawns. Human rights abuses against child combatants by rebel forces, particularly heinous or violent abuses, have been highlighted by governments, whereas similar abuses by government or pro-government forces have been concealed and denied.

Gender plays an important role in how violations of human rights are highlighted when it is to the advantage of the government, particularly with respect to the abduction, sexual enslavement, rape and sexual defilement of girls. Governments deny, conceal and manipulate information regarding their use and pro-government militias' use of girl and boy combatants; this is particularly true for girls. In order to prevent their visibility, governments attempt, and often succeed, in blocking entrance of these children into official government programs for ex-combatants or child combatants.

POLICY RECOMMENDATIONS
Governments, the United Nations, multilateral agencies and INGOs should

> Recognize that government emphasis on bringing international attention to the use of, and violence against, boy and girl combatants cannot be viewed simply as "humanitarian." Particular forms of gender-based violence and violence against girls by rebels are often highlighted by governments for political advantage, while almost no resources are put towards assisting them. This can result, in part, in a skewed understanding of girls' presence and experiences within fighting forces, contributing to analytic, operational and program errors.

> Recognize that in cases where the government is complicit in using child combatants, government child combatants may be blocked from entering any programs for ex-combatants. Consequently, children who gain entrance into DDR programs are unlikely to be representative of actual child combatant populations. In both UN and government DDR and reintegration programs for ex-combatant children, a negative bias exists against girls from all forces, but particularly with respect to government or pro-government forces.

> Remain vigilant in monitoring, investigating, reporting on and holding governments accountable for their use of child combatants.

Rights and Equity in DDR
FINDING:
Officials need to know the following about girls and young women in fighting forces and groups to plan effective and equitable DDR programs.

1. Numbers of girls within all fighting forces are routinely underestimated. This occurs in part because heavy emphasis on their roles as "wives," "sexual slaves" and "camp-followers" obscures their multiple and diverse roles. In particular, use of the term "camp-follower" obscures more than it reveals and should be avoided or used sparingly and with great caution (UN, 2002).

2. Female captives are often unable to leave their male captors for a variety of security, economic and logistical reasons.

3. Notions of childhood are defined by local legal and customary standards and practices and often do not parallel international legal definitions or the age-based restrictions used by some UN agencies or INGOs. Bias exists against women who enter or are abducted into the armed forces as girls, including the characterization of girls in fighting forces, because those staying past age 17 are often excluded from sampling. Another example is classifying girls who are married with babies as "women." Notably, locally-based NGOs and community-based organizations in all three countries did not use age-based restrictions in determining eligibility of young people from the fighting forces into their programs and directed their programs more holistically to affected populations.

4. Having DDR processes planned and implemented by military officials has resulted in bias against those the military does not consider "real soldiers" (i.e., men with guns). Requirement of a weapon for entry (or confusion about this requirement) discriminates against children in general and girls and young women in particular.

5. Emphasis on attracting predominately armed males to areas to disarm and demobilize them exists at the cost of providing secure environments for women and girls in or associated with fighting forces. Poorly designed and crowded demobilization centres and ICCs present particular security risks for females.

6. Material provisions for girls within demobilization centres are not adequate, especially regarding hygiene materials (including soap, shampoo, oil and materials for menstruation) and clothing.

7. Operating child combatant programs under the larger umbrella of programs for "separated children" has a number of benefits, including demilitarizing programs and reducing stigma and community anger over privileging one group of children over another. However, these programs can serve as a barrier to addressing the needs of children not thought to be separated from their families, such as those associated with local militias.

8. Access to schooling in ways that encourage the community to accept ex-combatants into the schools and communities is essential. Mediation work among communities and teachers should be a central part of assisting children to reintegrate.

POLICY RECOMMENDATIONS
Governments, the United Nations, multilateral agencies and INGOs involved in DDR should

> Ensure that all peace negotiations and accords recognize the needs and rights of child soldiers and children in the fighting forces, including girls and young women, and plan for their demobilization and reintegration into community life.

> In conflicts that involve child soldiers, start from the assumption that girls are present in fighting forces, comprising anywhere from 10 to 33 percent of children in fighting forces.

> Increase efforts to demilitarize demobilization programs for children. Children should be removed from military exposure as quickly as possible. Guns or weapons should never be required to serve as a ticket for a child to receive demobilization benefits.

> Recognize that captive females face a series of security, economic and logistical constraints to "leaving" their captors. To help ensure their security, benefits and programs designed for these girls should not make their remaining with or leaving their captors a factor in amount of assistance received.

> Consult with gender experts in national and international humanitarian organizations and grassroots and national women's organizations for the development of secure camps for women, girls and boys. Develop clear policies for providing girls with proper hygiene materials (including for menstrual hygiene) and clothing at demobilization centres. UNICEF should take the lead in ensuring that NGOs operating ICCs are providing girls with these materials.

PROGRAM RECOMMENDATIONS
Governments, the United Nations, multilateral agencies and INGOs involved in DDR should

> Ensure that benefits for children in fighting forces include access to education or skills training with basic literacy and numerical training. Examples of such programs are UNICEF's community-based education programs in Sierra Leone.

> Ensure that programs for both education and skills training take into consideration that most children in fighting forces lack access to adequate food, particularly in the case of girl mothers. Wet feeding[31] at schools and skills centres encourages the attendance of girl mothers and provides them and their children with at least one meal a day. Access to food for themselves and their children can make a difference as to whether some girl mothers participate in the sex trade, either occasionally or regularly.

From Margin to Centre: Girls and Young Women in Fighting Forces

There are many more girls involved in fighting forces and as fighters than have previously been acknowledged. In the countries we studied, girls reported being a fighter as one of their top two to three primary roles. Depending on the country, between half to nearly all of them were trained to fight and expected to fight if called upon, including those who were pregnant and/or had small children.

Therefore, agencies and troops encountering such armed opposition forces, government sponsored militias, and, to a lesser extent, government forces, need to anticipate that girls and young women are likely to be among the fighters, including pregnant females and their small children. Girls and young women will likely also be among the porters carrying weapons, those sent in advance as sentries and those charged with caring for the wounded. In their tactics, facilities, supplies and programs, military forces fighting against and holding such children and youth are bound by international humanitarian law to make necessary provisions and plans for care of these females. Recognition and planning for girls and young women in fighting forces also need to be a top priority for local NGOs, local grassroots organizations, child protection agencies, regional and UN peacekeeping forces and DDR programs.

---

[31] Preparation and distribution of food on site.

The vast majority of these girls and young women did not enter fighting forces willingly but were abducted or "joined" as a matter of survival when no other option for protection was available. The failure of the state to protect its citizens from predatory forces, including rebels and government-supported militias, means that children and youth are easy targets for abduction and forced recruitment. Likewise, the failure of the state to provide adequate food, shelter, livelihood options and educational opportunities also motivates some children and youth to join armed opposition groups, militias and government forces.

Significantly, many rebel groups that make use of children and youth consider them as war slaves. They are war slaves because they do not join of their free will, nor can they leave, and they are only minimally fed and clothed (see Bales, 2000). They take very little to maintain because they are viewed and treated as expendable, to the point of being left to die from their wounds because using medicine on them is considered a waste.

They generate high profits for their commanders through looting and activities in illicit war economies, and it is their productive and reproductive labour that forms the backbone of many of today's rebel forces. They raid for and grow food, acquire medical supplies, fetch water, serve as porters, care for the wounded and provide information to plan future attacks. They supply the labour needed to extract diamonds, gold and other minerals, cut timber, and load trucks and planes so that the war economies that make up and fuel today's armed conflicts can function. They are used to carry out the most violent attacks, which tear the fabric of their communities and nations. They fight and are killed.

Recognizing this, issues of children and youth in fighting forces move from the margins to the centre in understanding today's armed conflicts. Children and youth make up more than half of many of the fighting forces. Thus, from the local to the international level, those seeking to understand and address the most pressing issues arising from today's armed conflicts will need to carefully reflect on the central role played by girls and boys in these fighting forces and conflicts and what it means in terms of intervention, assistance and the future of the countries involved.

6 Conclusion: Seeing Girls in Fighting Forces

At its core, this study's findings emphasize the implications of *seeing* girls in fighting forces. It is these implications that provide a vision to help inform and shape future actions.

The first implication is that Western notions of "child" and "childhood" need to be re-conceptualized in context; at best such notions are unhelpful, at worst, they are exclusionary. But the solution is not to simply embrace non-Western notions of childhood that are linked to rites of passage or particular actions, although such understandings are foundational to working successfully with these girls, young women and their communities.

Rather, we need to come to terms with the fact that in none of the countries and cultures we worked in were the more extreme actions that these girls and young women carried out part of the culture for children *or* adults. Being forced to drink water from human skulls, eating human flesh, collecting bags of ears and hands, being forced to be a "wife" to a man with over 20 other captive wives, beating your teachers or neighbours to death, killing your parent or sibling, torturing your colleagues—none of these actions can be understood, addressed or remedied within a framework or context of "childhood" or "adulthood."

What is needed is an understanding that participation in these actions and individual's responses to their participation will have an impact on more than the individual or even her community. It will move the society itself in different directions. In trying to support healing of these girls and young women and their communities, we saw that religious, spiritual and traditional leaders had modified or created rituals, since they had not encountered such realities before. We will need to listen carefully to and think hard about the stories they and their communities tell in order to gain a better understanding of the very new spaces these girls and young women are occupying *and* the ways in which, willingly or not, their societies are forced to move into these spaces with them.

The second major implication is recognition that the vast majority of these girls and young women have suffered severe violations of their human rights and have witnessed and, in some cases, participated in acts of extreme violence. Despite this, they show tremendous ability to calculate and cope. Most of us would be hard-pressed to survive the situations many of these girls have gone through. At the same time, it is essential that the coping strategies and resilience demonstrated by them not be mistaken for empowerment.

Girls and young women clearly articulate what is empowering to them. What is empowering to them, they tell us, is acceptance in their communities, the love and support of their families, friends whom they can rely on and rituals to reaffirm that they are useful and wanted, that they are forgiven, and that they are cleansed. We learned that in communities that assist them, the rituals and acceptance continue as a process in which the girls and young women are constantly told, in many ways in daily interactions with their peers and community members, that they are valued members of that community.

Girls overwhelmingly cite access to education, which helps them see a broader and brighter future, and training in skills that will enable them to contribute to or support themselves and their families. Of crucial importance also are their health and access to medicine and treatment for STDs, injuries and illnesses. Health care, especially reproductive health care, is a critical priority. Girl mothers and their children are at the greatest risk of not being accepted into their communities, of not having access to education or skills training and of being in poor health. As a cohort, they need to be prioritized for assistance.

We see clearly that the role of the community's women is central to these processes and that often they are gendered. Without them, girls and young women have greater difficultly reintegrating and moving forward in their lives. Thus, including women's knowledge and expertise, which exists within their communities, is vital to building up girls' and young women's self-confidence, self-esteem and capabilities. It is also vital in helping girls grow into useful members of their communities and nations and to become strong women leaders, like those who are now assisting them. Consequently, local, national and international organizations must continue to find ways to support and enhance the work of local women and local women's organizations.

A third implication is that taking seriously girls' roles and experiences in fighting forces leads to a deeper understanding of what it takes to create and maintain the kinds of fighting forces and armed conflicts we are now seeing. To begin with, we need to recognize that gender is a key factor, perhaps the key factor, in maintaining fighting forces (see Enloe, 2000). To illustrate, it is clear that women's and girls' labour in the fighting forces we studied was not incidental, but in most cases was the foundation upon which the fighting forces relied. This is particularly true for armed opposition or rebel forces, since they cannot rely on state structures and inputs to maintain their forces.

Recognizing this means that we should anticipate that girls and young women will be among the last to be released by the fighting forces, if indeed they are released at all. One only needs to look at the numbers of child soldiers released by rebels to see that girls and their labour are prized possessions, not easily or willingly parted with. For example, between May 20 and May 29, 2001, in a sign that they were willing to talk peace, the RUF released 1088 boys, but only 15 girls (Mazurana, McKay, Carlson, and Kasper, 2002).

Those trying to secure the release of children must put the issue of gender squarely on the table in negotiations with commanders. They will need to have as clear an understanding as possible about how gender functions in the country and cultures they are working in and how those gender roles have been manipulated, and in some cases expanded, to help maintain the fighting forces. Most importantly, they will have to come to terms with the importance, indeed, centrality, of girls' and women's productive and reproductive labour within those forces. If they can understand this, they have a much better chance of gaining the release of these girls and young women and potentially preventing future recruitment and abduction.

One step in the right direction of recognizing girls' and young women's centrality in fighting forces would be to discard the simplistic notion of "camp followers," as it does not assist in understanding the numerous roles and dimensions of girls' and young women's involvement in today's fighting forces. In the course of our work, it became increasingly clear to us that women, girls and their children were all too often categorized as "camp followers" by military, government and aid officials, who would rather not be responsible for them. As such, they were lumped into a category that made it appear that these females were "not really" part of the fighting forces. Our research shows this to be a serious miscalculation (see also UN, 2002).

The fourth implication is an understanding that girls' roles and experiences in fighting forces are multifaceted and complex. At times they are simultaneously victims and perpetrators. Thus, limiting our understanding of the roles these girls play to those of victims, "sexual slaves," or "captive wives" should be avoided as it leads to conceptual, policy and programmatic errors. While it is true that these girls were victimized, they are now moving on with their lives. Their experiences have taught them both positive and negative lessons that they may selectively return to as they confront future challenges.

Rather than starting from a place of "healing a victim," with a notion of regaining a norm that will never be regained, a need exists for a holistic approach to dealing with these girls and young women, one that takes into account the gendered physical, psychological, spiritual and social aspects of healing and reintegration. For example, girls who are physically and or psychologically unwell cannot receive the full benefits of participating in skills training or education. Girls whose families reject their children find it very difficult to access and benefit from skills training or educational opportunities, due to lack of child care.

At the same time, this holistic approach must take into account the very real economic and political context in which these girls live and seek to make their lives. The kinds of labour opportunities that exist for them, how the conflict has affected their local economies, the kinds of coping strategies being used by other members of the community to survive, and how the current political situation impacts their community and region must be key issues factored in and addressed. Such an approach necessitates a gendered understanding of the social, economic and political context these girls live in, and an understanding of the ways those gender dimensions are being pushed by both progressive and repressive forces in the country and, indeed, often by the girls themselves.

A holistic approach would ideally work in tandem with the efforts of the men and women who make up communities—not only leaders, but parents, relatives and neighbours. Girls and young women who return to their communities need to be able to see that there are adults in their lives who will have a positive influence over them, and that they will no longer be controlled by violent men, as they were during captivity. They need to see that, although they have changed, they have a place and a future in the community they have returned to, and that they can make meaningful contributions to that community.

References

Abdullah, Ibrahim. 1998. *Bush path to destruction: The origin and character of the Revolutionary United Front [RUF]/Sierra Leone.* Journal of Modern African Studies. 36: 203-235.

Agger, Inger. 1994. *The blue room: Trauma and testimony among refugee women, a psycho-social exploration.* London: Zed Books.

Amnesty International. 1997. *Uganda: "Breaking God's commands": The destruction of childhood by the Lord's Resistance Army.* New York: Author.

AI. 1999. *In the firing line: War and children's rights.* London: Amnesty International UK.

AI. 2001. *Guinea and Sierra Leone: No place of refuge.* London: Author.

Angulo, Joy. June 2000. *Gender, abduction and reintegration in Northern Uganda.* (Occasional Paper No. 6). Kampala, Uganda: Makerere University, Department of Women's Studies.

Arnston, Laura and Neil Boothby. 2002. *"A world turned upside down"—child soldiers in Mozambique: A case study of their reintegration.* Unpublished manuscript. Washington, DC: Save the Children Federation, U.S.

Bales, Kevin. 2000. *Disposable people: New slavery in the global economy.* Berkeley: University of California Press.

Bangura, Yusuf. 2000. *Strategic policy failure and governance in Sierra Leone.* Journal of Modern African Studies.

Barth, Elise F. 2003. *Peace as disappointment: The reintegration of female soldiers in post-conflict societies: A comparative study from Africa.* Oslo: Peace Research Institute, Oslo. Available online at http://www.prio.no/publications/reports/femalesoldiers

Barton, Tom, Alfred Mutiti and the Assessment Team for Psycho-social Programmes in Northern Uganda. 1998. *Northern Uganda psycho-social needs assessment report.* Kisubi: Marianum Press.

Bernard, Russell. 2002. *Research methods in anthropology: Qualitative and quantitative methods,* 3rd edition. Oxford, England: Rowman and Littlefield.

Bond, George C. and Nigel C. Gibson (Eds.). 2002. *Contested terrains and constructed categories: Contemporary Africa in focus.* Boulder, Colorado: Westview Press.

Brett, Rachel. December 2002. *Girl soldiers: Challenging the assumptions.* Child Soldiers Newsletter No. 6: 7-9.

Brownmiller, Susan. 1975. *Against our will: Men, women, and rape.* New York: Simon and Schuster.

Carpenter, R. Charlie. 2002. *Assessing and addressing the needs of children born of forced maternity.* Background papers, The International Conference on War-Affected Children, Winnipeg, Manitoba, Canada, September 10-17, 2000.

CCF Team in Angola with Alcinda Honwana. June 1998. *'Okusiakala Ondalo Yokalye' Let us light the fire: Local knowledge in the post-war healing and reintegration of war-affected children in Angola.* Unpublished manuscript.

Charfi, M.. 1996. *Assistance to Somalia in the field on human rights – report of the independent expert, Mr. M. Charfi, on the situation of human rights in Somalia.* New York: United Nations.

Chingono, Mark. 1996. *The state, violence, and development: The political development of war in Mozambique, 1975-1992.* Hong Kong: Aveberry.

Coalition to End the Use of Child Soldiers [Coalition]. 2000a. *Americas report.* Available online at www.childsoldiers.org/americas

Coalition. 2000b. *Africa report.* Available online at www.childsoldiers.org/africa

Coalition. 2000c. *Asia report.* Available online at www.childsoldiers.org/asia

Coalition. 2000d. *Europe report.* Available online at www.childsoldiers.org/europe

Coalition. 2000e. *Special report: Girls with guns.* Available online at www.childsoldiers.org/reports/special%20reports

Coalition. 2001. *Child soldiers global report.* London: Author.

Coalition. 2002, November 7-9. *Report: Great Lakes Strategy Workshop.* Nairobi, Kenya: School of Monetary Studies.

Cock, Jacklyn. 1993. *Women and war in South Africa.* Cleveland, Ohio: Pilgrim Press.

Cohn, Ilene. and G. Goodwin-Gill, 1994. *Child soldiers: The role of children in armed conflict.* Oxford: Clarendon Press.

De Pauw, L. G. 1998. *Battle cries and lullabies: Women in war from prehistory to the present.* Norman: University of Oklahoma Press.

Djeddah, Carol. 1997. *Wars and unaccompanied children in Africa: Who they are and major health implications.* International Child Health, 8 (2). Available online at www.ipa-france.net/pubs/inches/inch8_2/djed.htm

Draisma, Frieda, and Eunice Mucache. April 23-30, 1997. *Physical and psychological recovery and social reintegration of child soldiers: The experience of Mozambique.* Symposium on the prevention of recruitment of children into armed forces and demobilization and social reintegration of child soldiers in Africa. Cape Town, South Africa.

Edgerton, Robert B. 2000. *Warrior women: The Amazons of Dahomey and the nature of war.* Boulder, Colorado: Westview Press.

Efraime, Boia Jr. and Antoinette Errante. n.d. *Rebuilding hope on Josina Machel Island.* Unpublished manuscript.

Enloe, Cynthia. 2000. *Maneuvers: The international politics of militarizing women's lives.* Berkeley: University of California Press.

Errante, Antoinette. 1999. *Peace work as grief work in Mozambique and South Africa: Post-conflict communities as context for child and youth socialization.* Peace and Conflict: Journal of Peace Psychology. 5: 261-279.

Femmes Africa Solidarité. 2000. *Engendering the peace process in West Africa: The Mano River women's peace network.* Geneva: Cavan S.A., Grandson.

Finnstrom, Sverker. 2001. *In and out of culture: Fieldwork in war-torn Uganda.* Critique of Anthropology. 21: 247-258.

Francis, David J. 2000. *Torturous path to peace: The Lomé Accord and postwar peacebuilding in Sierra Leone.* Security Dialogue. 31: 357-372.

Honwana, Alcinda. 1997. *Healing for peace: Traditional healers and post-war reconstruction in Southern Mozambique.* Peace and Conflict: Journal of Peace Psychology. 3: 293-305.

Honwana, Alcinda. 2001. *"Children of war: Understanding war and war cleansing in Mozambique and Angola."* In *Civilians in war.* Edited by Simon Chesterman. Boulder, Colorado: Lynne Reinner. 123-142.

Human Rights Watch [HRW]/Africa Watch. 1992. *Conspicuous destruction: War, famine and the reform process in Mozambique.* New York: Author.

HRW/Africa/ HRW Children's Rights Project. 1994a. *Easy prey: Child soldiers in Liberia.* New York: Human Rights Watch.

HRW/Africa/ HRW Children's Rights Project. November 1994b. *Sudan: The lost boys: Child soldiers and unaccompanied boys in southern Sudan.* New York: Human Rights Watch.

HRW/Africa and HRW/Children's Rights Project. 1997. *The scars of death: Children abducted by the Lord's Resistance Army in Uganda.* New York: Author.

HRW. July 1998. *Sierra Leone: Sowing terror: Atrocities against civilians in Sierra Leone.* New York: Author.

HRW. June 1999. *Getting away with murder, mutilation, and rape: New testimony from Sierra Leone.* New York: Author.

HRW. January 2002. *We'll kill you if you cry: Sexual violence in the Sierra Leone conflict.* 15 (1A): 1-75.

HRW. March 2003. *Stolen children: Abduction and recruitment in Northern Uganda.* 15(7A): 1-24.

HRW. July 2003. *Abducted and abused: Renewed conflict in Northern Uganda.* New York: Author.

HRW/HRW Children's Rights Project. January 1996. *Children in combat.* New York: Human Rights Watch.

International Labour Office. April 2003. *Wounded childhood: The use of children in armed conflict in Central Africa.* Washington, DC: Vanguard Communications.

ISIS-WICCE. June 1998. *Documenting women's experiences in armed conflict situations in Uganda 1980-1986: Luwero District.* Kampala, Uganda: Author.

ISIS-WICCE. July 2001a. *Women's experiences of armed conflict in Uganda, Gulu district 1986-1999, Part I.* Kampala, Uganda: Author.

ISIS-WICCE. July 2001b. *Medical interventional study of war affected Gulu District, Uganda, Part II.* Kampala, Uganda: Author.

Jones, David. 1997. *Women warriors: A history.* Washington, DC: Brassey's.

Keairns, Yvonne. October 2002. *The voices of girl child soldiers.* NY and Geneva: Quaker UN Office.

Legrand, Jean-Claude. October 1999. *Lessons learned from UNICEF field programmes for the prevention of recruitment, demobilization, and reintegration of child soldiers.* New York: UNICEF.

Lindsey, Charlotte. 2001. *Women facing war.* Geneva: International Committee of the Red Cross.

Lorentzen, Lois A. and Jennifer Turpin. 1998. *The women and war reader.* New York: New York University Press.

Luciak, Ilja. 2001. *After the revolution: Gender and democracy in El Salvador, Nicaragua, and Guatemala.* Baltimore and London: Johns Hopkins University Press.

Machel, Graça. September 2000. *The Machel review document, the impact of armed conflict on children: Four years later, September 2000.* Background Papers: International Conference on War-Affected Children. Winnipeg, Manitoba, Canada.

MacMullin, Colin and Maryanne Loughry. April 2002. *An investigation into the psychosocial adjustment of former abducted child soldiers in Northern Uganda.* Field report submitted to International Rescue Committee.

Malan, Mark, Sarah Meek, Thokozani Thusi, Jeremy Ginifer and Patrick Coker. March 2003. *Sierra Leone: Building the road to recovery.* (Monograph 80). Pretoria, South Africa: Institute for Strategic Studies.

Manning, Carrie. 1998. *Constructing opposition in Mozambique: RENAMO as political party.* Journal of Southern African Studies. 24: 161-189.

Mazurana, Dyan and Susan McKay. 2001. "Women, girls, and structural violence: A global analysis." In *Peace, Conflict and Violence.* Edited by Daniel Christie, Richard V. Wagner and Deborah D.Winter. 130-138. Englewood Cliffs, New Jersey: Prentice Hall.

Mazurana, Dyan, Susan McKay, Khristopher Carlson, and Janel Kasper. 2002. *Girls in fighting forces and groups: Their recruitment, participation, demobilization and reintegration.* Peace and Conflict: Journal of Peace Psychology, 8: 97-123.

Mazurana, Dyan, and Susan McKay. September/October 2002. *Child soldiers: What about the girls?* Bulletin of the Atomic Scientists. 57(5): 31-35.

Mazurana, Dyan and Susan McKay. 1999. *Women and peacebuilding.*
  Montréal: Rights & Democracy (International Centre for Human Rights
  and Democratic Development).

McConnan, Isobel and Sarah Uppard. 2001. *Children, not soldiers.*
  London: Save the Children.

McKay, Susan. 1998. *The effects of armed conflict on girls and women.*
  Peace and Conflict: Journal of Peace Psychology, 4: 381-392.

McKay, Susan and Dyan Mazurana. September 2000. *Girls in militaries,
  paramilitaries, and armed opposition groups.* Background papers:
  International Conference on War-Affected Children, Winnipeg, Manitoba, Canada.

McKay, Susan and Dyan Mazurana. 2001. *Raising women's voices
  for peacebuilding: Vision, impact, and limitations of media technologies.*
  London: International Alert.

Ministry of Health and Sanitation, Sierra Leone, and International Rescue
  Committee Health Unit. 2001. *Mortality in Kenema district, Sierra Leone:
  A survey covering January 200-January 2001.* Freetown, Sierra Leone: Author.

Morrison, Andrew P. 1996. *The culture of shame.* New York: Ballantine Books.

Muhumuza, Robby. (nd). *Girls under guns: A case study of girls abducted
  by Joseph Kony's Lord's Resistance Army (LRA) in Northern Uganda.*
  Kampala, Uganda: World Vision, Uganda.

Nordstrom, Carolyn. 1997. *A different kind of war story.*
  Philadelphia: University of Pennsylvania Press.

Office for the Coordination of Humanitarian Affairs [OCHA]. February 24, 2003.
  Sierra Leone: Visit of UN Special Representative for Children.
  Accessed February 24, 2003: Integrated Regional Information Network [IRIN].

OCHA. March 28, 2003. *IRIN Interview on Disarmament, Demobilization,
  and Reintegration.* Accessed March 28, 2003: IRIN.

Physicians for Human Rights [PHR]. 2000. *March 2000 delegation to Sierra Leone:
  Preliminary findings and recommendations on the health consequences
  of human rights violations during the civil war.* Boston: Author

PHR. 2002. *War-related sexual violence in Sierra Leone.* Boston: Author.

Radda Barnen. 2002. *Africa report: Sierra Leone.* Accessed August 1, 2002:
  http://www.globalmarch.org/virtual-library/csucs/country-reports/
  africa/sierra_leone.htm

Refugees International. February 2002. *Children in the eastern Congo: Adrift in
  a sea of war and poverty.* Available online at www.refintl.org/cgi-bin/ri/bulletin

Rehn, Elisabeth and Ellen J.Sirleaf. 2002. *Women, war and peace: The independent
  experts' assessment of armed conflict on women and women's role in
  peacebuilding.* New York: United Nations Development Fund for Women.

Richards, Paul. 2001. "Are forest wars in Africa resource conflicts? The case of Sierra Leone." in *Violent environments.* Edited by Nancy Peluso and Michael Watts. Ithaca, New York: Cornell University Press. 65-82.

Richards, Paul. 1996. *Fighting for the rain forest: War, youth and resources in Sierra Leone.* Oxford: The International African Institute.

Rone, Jemera. July 29, 1998. *Crises in Sudan and Northern Uganda. Testimony before the House Subcommittee on International Operations and Human Rights and the Subcommittee on Africa.* Washington, DC.

Sajor, Indai L. 1998. *Common grounds: Violence against women in war and armed conflict situations.* Quezon City, Philippines: Asian Center for Women's Human Rights.

Save the Children [SC]. 2002. *HIV and conflict: A double emergency.* London: Author.

SC. 2003. *State of the world's mothers: Protecting women and children in war and conflict.* Available online at www.savethechildren.org/sowm2003/index

Sayagues, Mercedes. 2000. *Attitudes and knowledge about reproductive health and sex among Zambezia youth hinders HIV/AIDS and STDs awareness and education.* Global Information Network. Available online at www.globalinfo.org

Schaeller, Jane G. 1995. *Children, child health, and war.* International Child Health. 6 (4). Available online at www.ipa-france.net/pubs/inches/inch6_4/jane

Scheff, Thomas J. 1994. *Bloody revenge: Emotions, nationalism, and war.* Boulder, Colorado: Westview Press.

Shan Human Rights Foundation and Shan Women's Action Network. 2002. *Licence to Rape: The Burmese military regime's use of sexual violence in the ongoing war in Shan State, Burma.* Chiang Mai, Thailand: Author.

Shepler, Susan. (In Press). "Globalizing child soldiers in Sierra Leone." In Popular cultures, national ideologies, global markets. Edited by S. Maira and E. Soep. Philadelphia: University of Pennsylvania Press.

Shepler, Susan. 2002. *Les filles-soldats : Trajectoires d'après-guerre en Sierra Leone.* [Girl soldiers: Post-war trajectories in Sierra Leone] Politique Africaine. 88: 49-62.

Sommers, M. 1997. *The children's war: Towards peace in Sierra Leone. A field report assessing the protection and assistance needs of Sierra Leonean children and adolescents.* Available online at www.intrescom.org/wcwrc/reports/wc_sierra_leone

Stravrou, Stavros and Robert Stewart, with Amanda Stravrou. September 10-17, 2000. *The re-integration of child soldiers and abductees: A case study of Palaro and Pabbo, Gulu District, Northern Uganda.* Background papers: International Conference on War-Affected Children. Winnipeg, Manitoba, Canada.

Temmerman, Els de. 2001. *Aboke girls: Children abducted in northern Uganda.* Kampala, Uganda: Fountain Publishers.

Thompson, Carol. 1999. *Beyond civil society: Child soldiers as citizens in Mozambique.* Review of African Political Economy. 80: 191-206.

United Nations. 1995. *Beijing Platform for Action.* New York: Author.

UN. 1996. *The impact of armed conflict on children: Report of the expert of the Secretary-General, Ms. Graça Machel.* New York: Author.

UN. 2002. *Women, peace and security: Study of the United Nations Secretary-General as pursuant Security Council Resolution 1325.* New York: Author.

United Nations Children's Fund [UNICEF]. April 30, 1997. Cape Town annotated principles and best practices. Adopted by the participants in the Symposium on the Prevention of Recruitment of Children into the Armed Forces and Demobilization and Social Reintegration of Child Soldiers in Africa, organized by UNICEF in cooperation with the NGO Sub-group of the NGO Working Group on the Convention on the Rights of the Child, Cape Town.

UNICEF. 2002. *The state of the world's children 2003.* New York: Author.

UNICEF. (Unpublished Report). *Lessons learned in prevention, demobilization and reintegration of children associated with the fighting forces: A Sierra Leonean case study.*

UNICEF Eastern and Southern Africa Regional Office. October 10-12, 2001. *Executive Summary, Interagency meeting on demobilization of child soldiers in active combat.* Nairobi, Kenya.

UN High Commission on Refugees [UNHCR], and Save the Children-United Kingdom [SC-UK]. February 2002. *Sexual violence and exploitation: The experience of refugee children in Guinea, Liberia, and Sierra Leone: Initial findings and recommendations from Assessment mission 22 October to 30 November 2001.* New York: UNHCR.

UN Programme on HIV/AIDS [UNAIDS]. 2002. *Report on the global HIV/AIDS epidemic.* Geneva: Author.

UNAIDS. May 1998. *AIDS and the military: UNAID's point of view, UNAID's best practice collection.* Geneva: Author.

Veale, Angela. January 2003. *From child soldier to ex-fighter, a political journey: Female fighters, demobilization and reintegration in Ethiopia.* Unpublished report.

Veale, Angela and Aki Stavrou. November 2002. *Reintegration of former Lord's Resistance Army child soldier abductees into Acholi society.* Pretoria, South Africa: Institute for Security Studies.

Vines, Alex. 1991. *RENAMO: Terrorism in Mozambique.* London.

Wessells, Michael and Carlina Monteiro. 2003. "Healing, social integration, and community mobilization for war-affected children: A view from Angola." In *The psychological impact of war trauma on civilians.* Edited by Stanley Krippner and Teresa McIntyre. Westport, Connecticut: Praeger. 179-191.

Wilson, Kenneth. 1992. *Cults of violence and counter-violence in Mozambique.* Journal of Southern African studies. 18: 527-582.

Women's Commission for Refugee Women and Children. 2001. *Against all odds: Surviving the war on adolescents, promoting the protection and capacity of Ugandan and Sudanese adolescents in Northern Uganda.* New York: Author.

Women's Commission for Refugee Women and Children. 2002. *Precious resources: Adolescents in the Reconstruction of Sierra Leone.* New York: Author.

World Health Organization. 2003. *Mental health in emergencies: Mental and social aspects of health of populations exposed to extreme stressors.* Geneva: Department of Mental Health and Substance Dependence, World Health Organization.

World Vision. 1996. *The effects of armed conflict on girls: A discussion paper prepared by World Vision for the UN study on the impact of armed conflict on children.* Monrovia, California: Author.

Zapata, B.C., A. Rebolledo, E. Atalah, B. Newman and M.C. King. 1992. *The influence of social and political violence on the risk of pregnancy complications.* American Journal of Public Health. 82: 685-690.

Appendices

Appendix 1: Methodology

World-Wide Data
Data Gathering, Management and Analysis

Drawing on scholarly, governmental, non-governmental and United Nations (UN) documents, and interviews with key contacts, Mazurana investigated and analyzed the following for the years 1990–2003: a) global presence of girls in fighting forces, with specific data on country, name of force or group, and relevant dates; b) active recruitment of girls into fighting forces, including information on recruitment practices; c) information on joining practices of girls into fighting forces ; information on abduction and gang pressing of girls into fighting forces; and d) roles girls play within fighting forces during armed conflict.

To compile these data, three independent sources were located that could confirm the presence of girls in the fighting forces in the particular country. In most cases, the sources of information were produced by international child rights' NGOs, newspaper articles, reports sent to or produced by the UN or humanitarian aid organizations, and correspondence with humanitarian officials within the UN and INGOs. Mazurana designed topical coding systems and databases for recording findings from each region of the world in Microsoft Word© software (for discussion of topical coding, see Bernard, 2002). Research assistants helped locate sources of information on girls in fighting forces, coded them, and entered the data. Mazurana checked all entered data for quality, tabulated data, and used the findings to produce a series of maps and tables to present them.

Northern Uganda, Sierra Leone and Mozambique

For the CIDA/ Rights & Democracy study, Dyan Mazurana and Susan McKay served as co-primary investigators. This section describes the data gathering and management and analytic methods used.

Data Gathering: Prior to fieldwork, Mazurana and McKay synthesized data by drawing upon scholarly, governmental, NGO and UN documents to obtain background material on the historical, political, economic and social contexts, and the impacts of the armed conflict on girls and women in Northern Uganda, Southern Sudan, Sierra Leone and Mozambique. Their understanding of these situations was enhanced by discussions with key individuals and contacts who work internationally and on the ground in these countries.

Interviews: Mazurana and McKay conducted 38 audiotaped semi-structured interviews during fieldwork in Uganda from November to December, 2001. McKay conducted 37 interviews from May to June, 2002 in Sierra Leone. Mazurana and Khristopher Carlson conducted 26 semi-structured interviews in Sierra Leone from August to September. Mazurana and McKay conducted 32 semi-structured interviews in Mozambique from September to October, 2001 (see Appendix 3 for details).

All interviews with girls were done in cooperation with NGO staff, social workers and/or psychologists. Study participants were familiar with those serving as interpreters for the interviews. In advance of their interviews with girls, the researchers explained the study to their interpreters and discussed the kinds of questions they might ask study participants. Most other interviews, such as with NGO staff and UN officials, took place in English.

Consent Process: Prior to beginning interviews, the researchers and/or interpreter explained the study to participants, including the study sponsorship, the purpose of the study, and why the individual was asked to participate. The researchers then explained the procedure of the interview, and that interview data and their identities would remain anonymous. Participants were told that they did not have to answer any questions they were uncomfortable answering, and they could end the interview at any time with no fear of penalty to themselves. No inducements were offered to the respondents prior to interviews that might influence their willingness to participate.

Quantitative Data: In Uganda, UNICEF provided quantitative data on numbers of children abducted. World Vision (WV) Uganda, Uganda Children of War Programme, Gulu, and GUSCO, Gulu, provided data on the number of children who pass through their centres as well as figures from the centre run by the Kitgum Concerned Women's Association, (KICWA), Kitgum.

In Sierra Leone, quantitative data on the fighting forces and their DDR, with particular emphasis on children and girls, were gathered from the Sierra Leone National Center for Disarmament, Demobilization and Reintegration (NCDDR) and UNICEF, Child Protection Unit, Sierra Leone.

In Mozambique, quantitative data include official disarmament, demobilization, and reintegration (DDR) figures on troop enrolment from the government of Mozambique and the UN. Mazurana and McKay also collected demographic and DDR data on 483 female combatants from FRELIMO and RENAMO from Maputo and Sofala provinces, compiled by the Association of Demobilized Soldiers (AMODEG). A comparison between Maputo and Sofala provinces allowed Mazurana and McKay to compare the FRELIMO stronghold, Maputo, with the RENAMO stronghold, Sofala. These data included force membership, location and age of entry, education level, health status, number and birth dates of children, specialty training, occupation within the fighting force, date of demobilization and reason for demobilization.

Data Management: Mazurana managed field notes and all but one audio transcript for Uganda, which was managed by McKay. Transcription of data from Uganda for 21 in-country interviews generated 196 pages. Mazurana transcribed 58 percent of the audiotaped interviews. For McKay's work in Sierra Leone, research assistant Maria Gonsalves managed field notes, and McKay managed all transcripts. All transcribed interviews were quality reviewed by McKay's research assistants. Transcription of data from Sierra Leone generated 705 pages; 100 percent of interviews were transcribed from audiotapes. For Mazurana and Carlson's work in Sierra Leone, Mazurana managed field notes and transcriptions. Eleven in-country interviews were transcribed from audiotapes and generated 84 pages. Data from 15 interviews were derived from field notes, generating 57 pages, for a total of 141 pages from Sierra Leone. Mazurana managed all field notes and transcripts for Mozambique. Transcription of data from Mozambique generated 294 pages; 84 percent of interviews conducted were transcribed from audiotapes. For the AMODEG data from Mozambique, Mazurana managed data files. Mazurana created a database using Excel© software and designed spreadsheet categories, Carlson entered data, and Mazurana quality checked data.

Data Analysis: Mazurana read all transcripts and field notes and identified the main categorical components within each, including age at entry into force, force name, entry routes, roles, training with the force, experiences of human rights violations within force, exit routes, disarmament, demobilization and reintegration. Mazurana then compared categorical data first by force and then by country. When possible, both force and country findings were compared to previously published data, including historical facts, to assist in checks for accuracy. Country findings were then comparatively analyzed among the three countries to develop overall findings.

For AMODEG data, Mazurana generated histograms and descriptive statistics in Excel©. A number of biases exist in the data from AMODEG, most related to how these data were collected by AMODEG—in particular the use of popular radio to call people to register and length of time between separation from force and date of registry (e.g., some people registered after having been five years out of the forces).

For McKay's study responsibilities, *a priori* coding categories were established to identify content from audiotaped transcripts to be analyzed. Coding categories were clustered within three broad thematic categories: Psycho-spiritual (9 codes), Sociocultural (8 codes), and Health (11 codes). Each code was operationally defined in writing by McKay for use by coders. Three research assistants, each conversant with issues related to gender and war, were trained in coding data. Each coded one of the three thematic categories for the 1336 pages of interview data entered into the Ethnograph© software. Bias occurred because analysis was limited to transcribed interview data that could be entered into the Ethnograph© software.

The bias is most apparent in the number of pages (705) generated from McKay's interviews in Sierra Leone that could be entered into the Ethnograph© in comparison with 294 pages (84 percent) transcribed for Mozambique, 196 pages (58 percent) for Northern Uganda, and 141 pages (100 percent) for Mazurana's CIDA/Rights & Democracy interviews in Sierra Leone. Thus analytic bias exists for McKay's Sierra Leone data set. McKay attempted to override some of this skew by consulting field notes for interviews that were not transcribed for the Northern Uganda and Mozambique fieldwork.

Three coders, each responsible for one major coding category, read the transcripts before beginning coding. Coders were inclusive rather than exclusive in coding data that did not explicitly fit into a category. Each coder wrote field notes during the coding process that contained questions, concerns, or assessments of data being coded. Coders met periodically with each other and McKay to discuss the coding process and data. Pages 5 and 10 of each interview transcript were cross-checked by two coders who were blind to each other's coding. Coding agreement was as follows: Psycho-spiritual 92.5 percent; Sociocultural 92.5 percent; Health 100 percent. Coded data were then entered into the Ethnograph© software program by research assistants and McKay. All coded data were then printed and organized into notebooks by thematic category and code to facilitate data analysis both within and between countries.

Using constant comparative and content analysis, McKay analyzed fourteen notebooks of coded data. Data for each coded category were analyzed both within and between countries. Detailed field notes organized around each code were kept. These notes were read and reread to increase understanding of emergent findings especially as they explicated cross-cutting themes across the three countries and country-distinct thematic content. Periodically, field notes were typed into a file of broad analytic observations. Nineteen pages of analytic notes were generated. Three levels of external review were then used:

a) First level review: Analytic notes were sent to external reviewers, who are CIDA study advisors, individuals from within the three field-site countries, experts in the field who are not study consultants, and two research assistants who worked closely with the study. Responses were received from nine individuals;

b) Second level review: McKay met for three and a half days in Laramie, Wyoming, USA with two expert consultants to discuss analytic notes and external reviews. She then wrote a semi-final draft of study findings and recommendations, which was reviewed and discussed by the on-site consultants and McKay and revised to be sent out for a third level of review;

c) Third level review: The third draft of study findings and recommendations was sent to external reviewers, three of whom had reviewed the initial analytic notes and two who had not. Three CIDA/Rights & Democracy study advisors were in this review group. Using their expert feedback, a final draft of findings and recommendations was developed.

Policy Commision Study of the Women Waging Peace Program Northern Uganda and Sierra Leone

With the approval of CIDA, Mazurana solicited funding from the PC, Washington DC and Cambridge, Massachusetts, USA, to enable more in-depth fieldwork than had been originally budgeted for in Sierra Leone, as well as a return trip to Northern Uganda in February, 2003. The PC study is parallel to the CIDA/Rights & Democracy study; findings are included in this paper in the country-specific findings for Northern Uganda and Sierra Leone because they expand upon the CIDA and Rights & Democracy study goals. Mazurana was the primary investigator and worked with research specialist Khristopher Carlson.

Data Gathering—Interviews: Semi-structured interviews and a structured survey were used for data gathering in Northern Uganda and Sierra Leone. Mazurana and Carlson interviewed 85 girls and young women associated with the LRA in Northern Uganda in February 2003. They conducted 42 interviews in Sierra Leone from August to September 2003. Mazurana and Carlson also interviewed community, traditional and religious leaders, parents of abducted girls and boys, and social and health workers who interact with the girls. The interview and consent process was similar to that described for the CIDA/Rights & Democracy study.

Surveys—Northern Uganda and Sierra Leone: A major data-gathering tool of the PC study was the use of surveys. Mazurana designed the surveys for Northern Uganda and Sierra Leone. She consulted with a biometrician about issues of sample size and the precision with which she could estimate percentages. She then obtained reviews from two practitioners before finalizing the design. The surveys in Northern Uganda and Sierra Leone were designed to use quota sampling.[32]

---

[32] Quota sampling was chosen as it was not possible for the researchers to do random sampling under the research conditions in Northern Uganda and Sierra Leone, because of challenges that included trying to locate populations that were mobile, girls wanting to remain unknown or who were in transit centres, poor communication and transportation conditions, as well as security risks throughout the countries. Therefore, Mazurana selected quota sampling because it is a type of sampling with results that approximate random sampling. In quota sampling, the researcher decides on the subpopulation of interest and other proportions of those subpopulations in the final sample. Next, the researcher identifies where the subpopulation can be found and selects members of the sample on the spot. The result is that although quota samples are biased, they often accurately reflect the population parameters of interest. The researcher then documents the bias in the sample (Bernard, 2002).

Northern Uganda

The Northern Uganda survey was designed as a quota sample of girls and young women formerly in the LRA during the war in Northern Uganda. Sub-categories of the study population included girl mothers who had become pregnant and or given birth while in captivity. Mazurana and Carlson selected study sites with the assistance of local and INGOs working in the North.[33] In most cases, the girls and women came to or were taken to these NGOs for assistance. In some cases, the girls had not come forward to the NGOs but were identified by NGOs as girls who had been associated with the LRA. The survey was conducted in February 2003, in the Gulu, Lira, and Apac districts in villages, trading centres, community centres, urban centres and reception centres. Mazurana and Carlson conducted all surveys working with interpreters who were known to the girls or young women. The survey contained 99 questions pertaining to basic demographic data, entry into the force, roles and experiences within the force, experiences of physical abuse within the respective forces and in community reintegration, experiences of time spent in the army barracks, official disarmament and demobilization, direct community entry, reintegration, skills training, assistance needs and current status. Fourteen open-ended questions were included in the survey itself; issues ranged from questions regarding why a girl joined an armed force if she reported joining, skills learned in fighting forces that could assist the respondent now, to difficulties and assistance during reintegration. All surveys were recorded on the survey form with additional details on any of the questions recorded in field notes.

For Mazurana and Carlson's study population of returnee[34] girls and young women from Northern Uganda (N=68), the precision of estimates is ± 0.12 for 10,000 female ex-combatants/returnees (95 percent confidence interval). There are biases in the study population. First, because of intense fighting, high levels of insecurity and concerns for researcher safety during the time the survey was being conducted in February 2003, slightly over half of the study population (53 percent) was drawn from the three relatively safe reception centres; thus, the findings are likely to over-represent participation in centres. Second, because pressure from Operation Iron Fist resulted in the LRA recently releasing captives, a higher number of girl mothers were taken to reception centres. Thus, the findings are likely to over-represent both numbers of girls with children and numbers of pregnant girls.

Study Population Overview: Descriptive data regarding Mazurana and Carlson's Northern Ugandan study population find that, at the time of interview, the mean and median age of the girls and young women was 17, with a range from 12 to 29. Half

---

[33] CPA, Uganda, a local NGO that works with former captive children and adults; WV, Uganda, an international NGO which runs a rehabilitation centre for children from throughout the North who were with the LRA; GUSCO, Gulu, a local NGO that operates a rehabilitation centre for children who were with the LRA from Gulu District; and Caritas House, Pader, an international NGO that operates a rehabilitation centre for children who were with the LRA from Pader District.

[34] Returnee refers to adults and children who were abducted into the LRA and have returned from captivity, including via escape, capture by Ugandan armed forces and other means.

of the study population was from the Acholi tribe and half were Lango. All reported abduction as the means of entry into the LRA, and 18 percent were abducted more than once. At the time of their abduction into the force, their mean age was over 12 and the median was 12, with a range of 7 to 23 years old. Ninety-three percent of the study population entered the LRA at under 18 years of age. The mean length of time in captivity was over four years, and the median length was four years—with some girls held for up to 12 years. The mean number of years of schooling was over four years and the median was five years, with a range from no schooling to 15 years. Seventy-four percent had received only primary schooling. Only six percent of the study population was married, either officially or common-law. At the time Mazurana and Carlson interviewed them, 16 percent had one child, 23 percent had two or more children, 1 percent had lost their only child, and 37 percent were currently pregnant. The largest percentage of girls (28 percent) named Lira District as their home district, followed by Pader District (21 percent), Apac (18 percent), Gulu (18 percent), and then Arua, Hoima, Kampala, Mbarara, and Moroto districts (1 percent each). Not surprisingly, given levels of internal displacement and insecurity, as well as the fact that our sample most likely over-represented girls in reception centres, 72 percent of the study population were outside of their original home districts at the time of interview.

Data Management and Analysis: Mazurana managed all field notes and survey data for the PC study. Data analysis of field notes was conducted by both Mazurana and Carlson and is similar to the process used by Mazurana in the CIDA/Rights & Democracy study. Working in Microsoft Excel©, Mazurana designed the database to analyze the surveys, Carlson entered the data, and Mazurana quality checked it. Mazurana then used histograms and descriptive statistics for initial analysis of the data.

Sierra Leone

The Sierra Leone survey was designed as a quota sample of girls and young women formerly in the fighting forces during the 1991–2002 war. Sub-categories of the study population included captive "wives" of commanders and girls involved in Civil Defence Forces (CDFs). Mazurana and Carlson selected study sites with the assistance of UNICEF in Sierra Leone and two international and two local NGOs working with child ex-combatants or war-affected communities in Sierra Leone.[35] In most cases, the girls and women came or were taken to these NGOs for assistance. In some cases, the girls had not come forward to the NGOs but were identified by community leaders to these NGOs as girls who had served in the fighting forces. The sampling took place in different geographical regions of the country and included

---

[35] IRC and COOPI were the INGOs and the two local NGOs were Caritas House, Makeni and Caritas House, Kenema.

the Western Area (the area including and surrounding the capital Freetown) and two of three provinces, the North and the East. Additionally, Mazurana and Carlson conducted surveys in a variety of locations, including remote villages, "suburbs" of urban centres, urban centres, and interim care and training centres for war-affected youth. The survey was conducted from August to September, 2002.

To enable comparative analyses, the Sierra Leone survey was similar to the Northern Uganda survey, with the exception that it included questions regarding participation in official DDR processes and skills-training programs and did not include questions regarding experiences in the barracks. Fourteen open-ended questions similar to those in the Northern Uganda survey were included.

For Mazurana and Carlson's study population in Sierra Leone (N=50) the precision of estimates is ± 0.14 for 10,000 female ex-combatants (95 percent confidence interval) and ± 0.2 for a population of 529 girls who went through disarmament and for a population of 507 girls who went through official demobilization conducted via Interim Care Centres (ICCs) (unpublished data provided to Mazurana and Carlson by UNICEF, Sierra Leone, 2002; NCDDR, Government of Sierra Leone, unpublished data provided to authors by NCDDR, 2002).

Mazurana and Carlson's study population in Sierra Leone is biased in several ways. First, NGO staff and community leaders could locate the females interviewed. Although we interviewed females who had not participated in official programs for child combatants (such as through DDR or via ICCs), our population was in some way known to the NGOs we worked with. Thus, we did not work with girls whom NGOs did not know or could no longer locate. For example, on some occasions, NGO workers were unable to locate girls they were responsible for; some of these girls had left the area and had been gone "unnoticed" for over six months. Second, the girls we interviewed within particular NGO programs were probably having positive experiences in these programs. We assume this because they were still in the programs and could be located. Third, the study population is positively biased towards female ex-combatants from the former rebel RUF and negatively biased towards those within the SLA and various CDFs. This is because girls within the RUF had priority in entry into programs. As this finding came to light, Mazurana and Carlson focused data collection on the group about which the least was known, the CDFs.

Study Population Overview: Descriptive data regarding Mazurana and Carlson's Sierra Leone study population reveals that, at the time of interview, the mean and median age of the girls and young women was 18, with a range from 10 to 35 years of age. The study population came from a variety of ethnic groups: Temne (42 percent), Mende (23 percent), Kono (13 percent), Fuler (10 percent), Limba (8 percent), Kru (2 percent), and Soso (2 percent). The majority (94 percent) came from Sierra Leone, with the others coming from Guinea (4 percent), and Liberia (2 percent). Eighty-four percent of the study population entered a fighting force when they were under 18 years of age. At time of their entry into the force, their mean age was 13 and the median was 12, with a range of 2 to 32 years old. Ninety-four percent reported abduction as means of entry into a fighting force; the remaining six percent reportedly "joined." The mean length of time in captivity was over three years and the median was three years, with some girls held for up to ten years. The mean years of schooling prior to entry into a fighting force was over two years and the median was zero, with a range from no schooling to nine years of school. Ninety percent had only received primary schooling, with 58 percent only completing Primary One (first grade). Thirty percent of the study population was married, officially or common-law, 24 percent had one child, and 8 percent had two or more children. Thirty percent had become pregnant during their time in the fighting force. The largest percentage of girls (58 percent) named the Northern Province as their home province, followed by the East (28 percent) and South provinces (12 percent). Twenty-four percent of the study population were outside of their original home province at the time of interview by Mazurana and Carlson.

Data Management and Analysis: Data management and analytical methods were identical to those used in the Uganda fieldwork described above.

Appendix 2: Why Think About Girls in Fighting Forces?

Our interest in learning more about what happens to girls in fighting forces began in the spring of 1999 when we were watching a videotape about a rehabilitation centre for child soldiers and the important work it was doing to help heal these children. For almost an hour, the video showed boys and activities structured for them. During the last five minutes, for the first time on the film, some girls were shown. Most of the girls had babies in their arms, and the video stressed that they were learning to be good mothers. The girls shown were all smiles. We both almost simultaneously spoke about the gender bias in the videotape, the lack of real information about girls, and their portrayal as happy mothers, even though these girls' pregnancies were undoubtedly the result of rape. Our discussion then progressed to issues about girls' human rights, gender discrimination, and the overall invisibility of girls within discourse about child soldiers. Thus, our study was born.

We obtained a small grant from the College of Arts and Sciences at the University of Wyoming to conduct an initial review of the extant literature on child soldiers and women and armed conflict. We found only a small amount of information—usually discussion of girls was embedded within internal NGO documents or UN reports of

DDR. Sometimes, as in the video that first piqued our interest, we noted photos of seemingly-happy mothers holding and smiling at their babies. In contrast to these representations, we talked with child protection advocates and human rights workers who were aware that girls were heavily used in fighting forces throughout the world, knew that their presence was largely hidden, and expressed concern that initiatives on their behalf were few.

When we presented our preliminary work in Winnipeg, Manitoba, Canada, in September 2000 at the International Conference on War-Affected Children, girls were occasionally mentioned within the larger discussion of child soldiers, for example by Graça Machel (2000), but, for the most part, boy soldiers were emphasized. With the financial support of CIDA in partnership with Rights & Democracy, we embarked on the CIDA study in March 2001. During this same period, a handful of international advocates were increasingly focusing upon girls' situations within fighting forces (for example, Keairns, 2002).

We began our fieldwork in Mozambique in the fall of 2001. During that war, girls in the fighting forces were virtually invisible, both within FRELIMO and RENAMO, and remain invisible to this day. Next, we conducted fieldwork in Northern Uganda, where knowledge about girls in armed forces was greater, heightened largely because of the Aboke school girls who were abducted by the LRA (Angulo, 2000) and where girls and boys are still abducted in large numbers by the LRA. During our fieldwork in Sierra Leone in 2002, we found that UNICEF and many NGOs were now recognizing that girls had been short-changed within DDR processes. Programs were being put into place to benefit girls, especially those girls abducted by the RUF. As of this writing, in both Northern Uganda and Sierra Leone, INGOs, local NGOs, grassroots groups and UN agencies are increasingly asking the question "What about the girls?" and are now developing initiatives and programs for them.

Yet, we still possess little systematic knowledge about girls' experiences and how best to work with them so that they and their children can live constructive lives. We hope this study begins to address some of the pressing issues faced by girls within the context of war in sub-Saharan Africa both thematically and by providing specific data gathered through interviewing girls in each country. Importantly, throughout this book, we have emphasized the importance of girls' human rights and the severe effects of sexism that exerts its influence both during and in the aftermath of armed conflict.

Appendix 3: Interviews

CIDA/Rights & Democracy Study
Number of girls interviewed by country

	Mozambique[36]	Uganda[37]	Sierra Leone[38]	Sierra Leone[39]	Total by category
Girls[40]	27	32	38	14	111
Young Women[41]	—	—	4	—	4
Mixed Group[42]	49	—	—	—	49
Total by Country	76	32	56		164

UN, Governmental, NGO and Grassroots Organization Interviews

MOZAMBIQUE
(Mazurana and McKay)

Place	Interviewees	Organization
Maputo, Mozambique	Agostinho Mamabe Renaldo Mucavebe	Association of Child, Family, and Development
Maputo, Mozambique	Duarte Joaquim	National Director of Women Sand Social Action
Maputo, Mozambique	Various board members	Board of AMODEG Demobilized Soldiers Association
Eduardo Mundalane University, Institute for Peace and Democracy	Joao Candido Pereira	Professor at Mundalane University
Ilha Joshina Machel, Mozambique	Bishop David Mahonza Timani	Saturday Church of Mozambique
Maputo, Mozambique	ICRC, Mozambique	ICRC
Beira, Mozambique	Madelana Sautor	Head of AMODEG Women's Division
Joshina Machel, Mozambique	Various activists	Joshina Machel Activists
Maputo, Mozambique	Boia Efraime Junior	Rebuilding Hope
Mozambique	Abu Sultan	Save the Children

36 Interviewed by Dyan Mazurana and Susan McKay.
37 Interviewed by Dyan Mazurana and Susan McKay.
38 Interviewed by Susan McKay and Maria Gonsalves.
39 Eight interviewed by Dyan Mazurana and Khristopher Carlson and six interviewed by Khristopher Carlson. Girls interviewed by Mazurana and Carlson for the Policy Commission study are not included in this table.
40 Under the age of eighteen.
41 Over the age of eighteen.
42 Mixed group, not able to distinguish who were abducted and who were not abducted.

UGANDA
(Mazurana and McKay)

Place	Interviewees	Organization
Kampala, Uganda	Eduard Sembidde	Save the Children, Denmark
Kampala, Uganda	Edith Nabiryo, Helen Namulwana, and various other female social workers	Hope After Rape
Kitgum, Uganda	CPA officers	CPA Kitgum Branch Office
Kitgum, Uganda	12 parents	CPA Lira Branch Office
Kitgum, Uganda	Angelina Atyam	CPA
Lira, Uganda	11 parents	CPA Lira Branch Office
Gulu City, Gulu	Paramount Chief	Acholi Paramount Chief
Apac, Uganda	LC5	LC5
Apac, Uganda	Seven parents	CPA Lira Branch Office
Lira, Uganda	Former Kony bodyguard	CPA Lira Branch Office
Gulu City, Gulu	Research officer	Research offices at GUSCO
Gulu City, Gulu	Outreach/Reintegration officer	World Vision Center
Gulu City, Gulu	Josephine Amogm	World Vision Center
Gulu City, Gulu	Various officers	UPDF CPU, Gulu District, 4th Division Battalion
Gulu City, Gulu	Florence Lakor	World Vision Center
Kampala, Uganda	Sandra Oder	Save the Children Denmark

SIERRA LEONE
(Susan McKay with Maria Gonsalves)

Place	Interviewees	Organization
Washington D.C.	Laura Arntson	Save the Children
Washington D.C.	Courtney Mireille O'Connor	Women's Commission for Refugee Women and Children
Freetown, Sierra Leone	Mohamed Abdul Kamara Reverend Sini	CAVE
Freetown, Sierra Leone	Reverend George Baunnie	CAVE
Freetown, Sierra Leone	Jeffrey Kyle Maureen Urquhart	Cause Canada
Freetown, Sierra Leone	Maude Peacock Yasmin Jusu-Sheriff	Truth and Reconciliation Commission
Freetown, Sierra Leone	Mabenti Bangura	Women's Awareness Movement
Freetown, Sierra Leone	May Williams	Cause Canada
Freetown, Sierra Leone	Donald Robertshaw Glenis Taylor	Child Protection of UNICEF
Freetown, Sierra Leone	Rugiatsu Turay Ibraham Kamara	Amazonian Initiative Movement

Freetown, Sierra Leone	Joe Alie Jebeh Forster Amy Juf Jeanne Harding	Truth and Reconciliation Commission
Freetown, Sierra Leone	Rev. Ayo McCauley	FAWE
Freetown, Sierra Leone	Antonio Piccoli Phillip Kamara Father Chema	Cooperazione Internazionale (COOPI)
Freetown, Sierra Leone	Davidson Jonah and staff	CCF
Freetown, Sierra Leone	Djanabou Mahonde	Deutsche Gesellschaft Für Technische Zusammenarbeit (GTZ)
Freetown, Sierra Leone	Catherine Wiesner	International Rescue Center
Freetown, Sierra Leone	Ibraham Sesay	Caritas-Makeni, Catholic Agency for Development and Relief
Freetown, Sierra Leone	Olayinka Laggah Charles Achodo	NCDDR
Makeni, Sierra Leone	Staff	Caritas Makeni
Makeni, Sierra Leone	Umu Turay	St. Joseph's School for the Deaf
Sierra Leone	Kadiata Bah Haja Sesay	Caritas-Makeni
Freetown, Sierra Leone	Binta Mansaray	Women's Commission for Refugee Women and Children
Cline Town, Freetown, Sierra Leone	Dr. Samuel Maligi II	Opportunities Industrialization Center
Freetown, Sierra Leone	Fonta Jabbe	Doctors Without Borders
Freetown, Sierra Leone	Christiana Thorpe	FAWE
Freetown, Sierra Leone	Foday Sawi	World Vision
Masiaka, Sierra Leone	Staff	CCF
Bo Town, Freetown, Sierra Leone	Hawa Kumba	War Affected Girls and Adults
Bo Town, Muluma	Hawa Bio	Women's Skills Development Association of World Vision
Bo Town, Sierra Leone	Nyama Kareno Jebe Sesay	IRC Skills Training Center
Bo Town, Sierra Leone	David Fortune Agnes Kumba Alfa Naba	IRC
Bo Town, Sierra Leone	Alfred Kamara	World Vision
Bo Town, Sierra Leone	Rose Marie Smith	World Vision
Calaba Town, Sierra Leone	Mameh Kargbo Victoria Finoubout Valeria Martyn	Cooperazione Internazionale (COOPI)
Freetown, Sierra Leone	Chris Robertson	Save the Children
Freetown, Sierra Leone	Rosaline McCarthy	Mano River Women's Peace Network
Abidjan, Ivory Coast, Sierra Leone	Andy Brooks	Save the Children
Cline Town, Sierra Leone	Fonta Jabee	Médecins sans frontières

SIERRA LEONE
(Dyan Mazurana)

Freetown, Sierra Leone	Francis Murray Lahai	Sierra Leone Ministry of Social Welfare
Port Loko, Sierra Leone	Esther A' Kamu	Caritas-Makeni
Koidu, Sierra Leone	Samuel "T-Boy" Tamba Kamanda	IRC
Yengema, Sierra Leone	Momoh Kpaka	IRC
Freetown, Sierra Leone	Olayinka Laggah	NCDDR
Freetown, Sierra Leone	Antonio Piccoli	Cooperazione Internazionale (COOPI)
Koidu, Sierra Leone	Alfred Sesay Matthew Sessay Mariamma Kabba	IRC
Port Loko, Sierra Leone	Ramatu Kamara	Caritas-Makeni
Port Loko, Sierra Leone	Michael Kamara	Caritas-Makeni
Makeni, Sierra Leone	R. Thoronka and F. Kamara	Reintegration for Caritas-Makeni
Koidu, Sierra Leone	Tamba Musa	NCDDR
Kenema, Sierra Leone	Amie Passay Samuel Turner	IRC
Koidu, Sierra Leone	Omar Keita	Progressive Women Association (PROWA) Training Institution
Freetown, Sierra Leone	Glenis Taylor	UNICEF
Port Loko, Sierra Leone	Ms. Bangora	Caritas-Makeni

Policy Commission Study

Number of girls surveyed and interviewed by country (Dyan Mazurana and Khristopher Carlson)

	Northern Uganda		Sierra Leone		Total by category
	Surveyed & Interviewed	Interviewed Only	Surveyed & Interviewed	Interviewed Only	
Girls (under 18 years of age)	43	17	24	17	101
Young Women (18 years of age and over)	25	—	26	—	51
Total by Country	85		61		146

UN, Governmental, NGO and Grassroots Organization Interviews/Policy Commission Study

SIERRA LEONE
(Dyan Mazurana and Khristopher Carlson)

Place	Interviewees	Organization
Freetown, Sierra Leone	Donald Robertshaw Keith Wright	UNICEF Child Protection
Freetown, Sierra Leone	Ibrahim Sesay	Caritas-Makeni
Freetown, Sierra Leone	Cynthia Kallay Philip Kamara	COOPI Data manager
Freetown, Sierra Leone	Shellac Davies	World Council of Churches
Freetown, Sierra Leone	Olayinka Laggah	NCDDR
Koidu, Sierra Leone	Komba Boima	NCDDR
Kenema, Sierra Leone	Samuel Turner Nancy Yoko Gender violence coordinator	IRC
Kenema, Sierra Leone	Mr. Sylvester Alfred Lansana	Caritas-Kenema
Kenema, Sierra Leone	Anonymous	Senior commander of Kamajors
Freetown, Sierra Leone	Aiah	Cooperazione Internazionale (COOPI)
Port Loko, Sierra Leone	Samuel Kamara	Caritas-Makeni
Port Loko, Sierra Leone	Anonymous	Senior commander of Gbethis
Freetown, Sierra Leone	Heidi Lehmann	IRC
Koidu, Sierra Leone	Dean Piedmont	IRC
Freetown, Sierra Leone	Gender-based violence and sexual exploitation officer	Office for the Coordination of Humanitarian Affairs, United Nations
Freetown, Sierra Leone	Foday Sawi	World Vision

NORTHERN UGANDA
(Dyan Mazurana and Khristopher Carlson)

Place	Interviewees	Organization
Kampala, Uganda	Eunice Oyet	CPA
Gulu City, Uganda	Dr. Frank Olyet	CPA
Gulu City, Uganda	Jo Becker Tony Tate	Human Rights Watch
Gulu City, Uganda	Grace Onyango, Director of Rehabilitation Centre Outreach Coordinator	World Vision
Gulu City, Uganda	Paul Rubangakene	Caritas-Pader
Gulu City, Uganda	Julius Tiboa Dora Alal Janet Renna	GUSCO
Lira, Uganda	Board of Directors Angelina Atyam	CPA, Uganda
Apac, Uganda	10 parents of abducted children Gender violence coordinator	CPA, Apac